RABBINIC JUDAISM'S GENERATIVE LOGIC

RABBINIC JUDAISM'S GENERATIVE LOGIC

VOLUME TWO

THE FORMATION OF THE JEWISH INTELLECT:
MAKING CONNECTIONS AND DRAWING CONCLUSIONS
IN THE TRADITIONAL SYSTEM OF JUDAISM

JACOB NEUSNER

Academic Studies in the History of Judaism
Global Publications, Binghamton University
Binghamton, New York
2002

Copyright © 2002 by Jacob Neusner

All rights reserved. No portion of this publication may be duplicated in any way without the expressed written consent of the publisher, except in the form of brief excerpts or quotations for the purposes of review.

Cover artwork by Suzanne R. Neusner.

Library of Congress Cataloging-in-Publication Data

Neusner, Jacob, 1932-
 Rabbinic Judaism's generative logic / Jacob Neusner.
    v. cm. -- (Academic studies in the history of Judaism)
 Includes bibliographical references.
 Contents: v. 1. The making of the mind of Judaism -- v. 2. The formation of the Jewish intellect, making connections and drawing conclusions in the traditional system of Judaism.
  ISBN 1-58684-181-5 (v. 1) -- ISBN 1-58684-182-3 (v. 2)
  1. Rabbinical literature--History and criticism--Theory, etc. 2. Judaism--Essence, genius, nature. 3. Judaism--History--Talmudic period, 10-425. 4. Tradition (Judaism)--History. I. Title. II. Series.
 BM496.5 .N48173 2002
 296.1'206'01--dc21
                                              2002001672

Published and distributed by:
Academic Studies in the History of Judaism
Global Publications, Binghamton University
State University of New York at Binghamton
LNG 99, Binghamton University
Binghamton, New York, USA 13902-6000
Phone: (607) 777-4495. Fax: 777-6132
E-mail: pmorewed@binghamton.edu
http://ssips.binghamton.edu and
http://globalpublicationspress.com

ACADEMIC STUDIES
IN THE HISTORY OF JUDAISM

Publisher: Global Publications, State University of New York at Binghamton
Address: LNG 99, SUNY-Binghamton, Binghamton, New York, 13902-6000

Editor-in-Chief

Jacob Neusner
Bard College

Editorial Committee

Alan J. Avery-Peck, *College of the Holy Cross*
Bruce D. Chilton, *Bard College*
William Scott Green, *University of Rochester*
James F. Strange, *University of Southern Florida*

TABLE OF CONTENTS

VOLUME TWO

THE FORMATION OF THE JEWISH INTELLECT: MAKING CONNECTIONS AND DRAWING CONCLUSIONS IN THE TRADITIONAL SYSTEM OF JUDAISM

PREFACE	ix
FOREWORD	xiii
VIII. THE FORMATION OF INTELLECT	1

PART ONE
TWO ISSUES IN THE ANALYSIS OF THE JEWISH INTELLECT

IX. THE MODALITY OF INTELLECT: SYSTEMATIC OR TRADITIONAL?	17

Part Two
Solutions and their Dilemmas

X.	Intelligible Discourse in Systemic Context: Pentateuchal Judaism	34
XI.	System and Cogency at Qumran	51
XII.	List-Making and System-Building in the Mishnah	75
XIII.	The Mixed Logics of Conclusion and Connection in the Traditional System of the Bavli	101

Part Three
The Conflict of System and Tradition: The Two Resolutions of the West

XIV.	Bavli vs. Bible. System and Imputed Tradition vs. Tradition and Imputed System	138

Volume One

The Making of the Mind of Judaism

Preface

Foreword

I. The Making of the Mind of Judaism

II. Ways Not Taken

III. A Preliminary Probe: The Four Logics of Sifré to Deuteronomy

IV. Propositional Discourse

V. META-PROPOSITIONAL DISCOURSE

VI. FIXED-ASSOCIATIVE DISCOURSE

VII. WHY NO SCIENCE IN THE MIND OF JUDAISM?

PREFACE

By "mind" or thought, I mean, specifically, the logic that generates new truth out of established fact. That generative logic dictates, first, how people connect one thing to something else, one fact to another, in literary terms, one sentence to another; and, second, the ways they form connections into large-scale conclusions, encompassing statements. Generative logic then determines how the result of connection generates large-scale construction of ideas. These two stages — the perception of connection between two things, the discernment of (self-evidently valid) conclusions based on the connection — characterize the normative mind of a culture. They further allow us to explore the potentialities and also the limitations of intellect, what people are likely to see or to miss. In these two volumes I explain how the authoritative, canonical documents of Rabbinic Judaism in its formative age signal the generative logic that animates all thought that is embodied in those writings.

This project treats as a continuous account of, and condenses two monographs on, the foundations of self-evidence in Rabbinic Judaism as represented by its formative canon, from the Mishnah through the Bavli. The two are as follows:

- *The Making of the Mind of Judaism.* Atlanta, 1987: Scholars Press for Brown Judaic Studies.
- *The Formation of the Jewish Intellect. Making Connections and Drawing Conclusions in the Traditional System of Judaism.* Atlanta, 1988: Scholars Press for Brown Judaic Studies.

The studies were connected, the second carrying forward the problem of the first, and they were meant to be read together and in sequence. There is a measure of overlap and some repetition, which I have tried to keep to a minimum. I omitted a chapter of the original *Formation* as well as a fair amount of illustrative material. But the two parts, while connected, do not repeat the main points. For first asks, in the context of the modes of constructive, coherent thought of the canonical writings, why no science in Judaism, such as the Mishnah could have sustained. For its part the second compares and contrasts the means of making connections and drawing conclusions of Judaism and Christianity, respectively: the one through the medium of the Talmud of Babylonia, the other through the medium of Scripture, thus, the Bavli versus the Bible.

The problem I address in asking about the generative logic of Rabbinic Judaism is simple: what are the rules of cogency, of coherent discourse, that everybody in the normative documents for granted, that is, what defines the self-evidence of the intellectual system of that Judaism? The Foreword of the first of the two parts of this project specifies what is at stake here: the intellectual basis on which the paramount Judaism of the ages engages, or does not engage, with the modern and contemporary sciences, democracy, capitalism, and philosophy. The Foreword of the second explains the comparison of the generative logics of several Judaisms, the Pentateuch, the system animating the Qumran Library, the Mishnah, the Talmud, and the Bible (that is, encompassing, as heir of Scripture, Christianity in the Bible).

I express my thanks to Professor David Ruderman, University of Pennsylvania, for his valuable reflections, in his work on science in

Judaism, on the original publication of *Making of the Mind* and this re-presentation of it in its larger monographic context.

I am further grateful to Global Publications for its publication of monographs of mine. Dr. Parviz Morewedge is a model of the academic entrepreneur, who makes possible the work of scholarship and its dissemination.

Jacob Neusner

Research Professor of Religion and Theology
Bard College
Annandale-on-Hudson, New York 12504
Neusner@webjogger.net

Foreword to
The Formation of the Jewish Intellect:

Making Connections and Drawing Conclusions in the Traditional System of Judaism

---

I now propose to account for how Judaic system-builders framed their systems in relationship to prior ones, beginning with the Pentateuchal system of Judaism. The formation of the Jewish intellect interprets the word "formation" in two senses. The first is "formation" as the ways in which that intellect formed a Judaic system, and the second is, "formation" as an account also concerning the structure of that intellect, that is, of what modes of thought that intellect was formed. First I want to know the order, proportion, structure, and composition of a Judaic system, that is, a world-view and way of life addressed to a defined social entity called (an) "Israel." Second, I propose to explain how framers of such a system made connections and drew conclusions in the setting up of their system. The order is deliberate. For I shall show that *the order of the formation of the intellect is from the whole to the parts.* The systemic statement defines the logic needed to make that statement. The manner of making connections and drawing conclusions does not percolate upward into the framing of the systemic statement.

At stake here is a long-term issue of culture, Judaic and Christian in antiquity, the relationship between system and tradition. Both religions claim to present enduring traditions, a fundament of truth revealed of old. But both religions also come to realization in systematic and philosophical statements, which begin in first principles and rise in steady and inexorable logic to final conclusions: compositions of proportion, balance, cogency, and order. And, not only so, but the systemic statements formed within both religions address not only problems of thought but the structure of society, explaining why people conduct their lives in one way, rather than in some other. Accordingly, a system-builder starts fresh to explain what is, in fact, the increment of the ages. Or so it would seem. And how people sort out the demands of a received belief in the confrontation with the fresh conceptions of a new day assuredly continues to enjoy the attention of religious intellectuals. Tradition and change, inherited ideas in tension with the reconstruction and re-visioning of a contemporary mind — these point to the ongoing relevance of the issue of the place system-builders make for themselves within a traditional order.

This work completes the inquiry begun in *the Making of the Mind of Judaism.* Having dealt with the logical structure of thought as revealed in one document, I now proceed to generalize on those results by comparing documents with one another. That involves moving out from the canonical writings of the Judaism of the Dual Torah to the systemic traits of other Judaisms that deal with the Pentateuch (in this analytical context including the Christianities that created the Bible). While this book and The Making of the Mind of Judaism therefore complement one another, each is meant be read on its own.

While the stakes are high and strikingly current, the issue of this book, spelled out in the Introduction, derives from the results of two completed monographs of mine. The one concerns the classification of thought as systematic or traditional, philosophical or historical in contemporary terms, the other, the description and analysis of modes of cogent discourse of a given system of thought. One step forward taken here is to deal at once with both questions in analyzing a broad range of Jewish writing from the Pentateuchal mosaic, ca. 500 B.C., through the Bavli, ca. A.D. 600, a period of nearly eleven hundred years. For when I asked about the classification of thought, I did not see the pertinence or uses of modes of cogent discourse, that is, the classification of what I call logics, in the analysis. And when I dealt with those logics, I did not grasp that they form an integral expression of the character of the document to which they impart composition and cogency as the interior structure of thought. But when I put the two distinct matters together, I found it possible to explain, from yet another perspective, what I deem to be the central trait of the Judaism of the Dual Torah, oral and written, that came forth from ancient times and constituted the normative Judaism of nearly the whole world from that time to the present. Let me state my simple proposition with heavy emphasis: It is the power of the Judaism of ,the Dual Torah in its statement in the Talmud of Babylonia or Bavli, to present as tradition what is in fact a system. This book explains the secret of that remarkable intellectual feat, and, in my view, provides yet another explanation for the single indicative trait of Judaism: the ubiquitous centrality and the paramount authority of a single document, the Talmud of Babylonia or Bavli. At the same time I show that an entirely unrelated set of intellectuals addressed the counterpart of the problem facing the Bavli's framers and solved it in a quite different way. Receiving a vast heritage of sacred writings, all of them in the status of tradition but none of them closely related to any other, the intellectuals who created the Bible, that is, the Old and New Testaments as a single book for Christianity, formed out of traditions a whole and cogent system. In late antiquity, two modes of dealing with the tension between tradition and system therefore emerged, the Judaic and the Christian, and both continued to serve the West, and indeed serve very well today.

II

Here I tell the story of how a well-composed and powerfully framed mode of deliberation, a manner of seeing things one way rather than some other, — again, a particular logic, or, as we shall see, blend of logics — took shape in the formative age of the Judaism of the Dual Torah that has constituted Judaism from the seventh century to our own time. That manner of seeing things, in particular told people how to make connections between one thing and another and drew and composed in large-scale constructions the conclusions dictated by those connections, which is to say, how to make sense of detail and hold the whole together. My claim to describe, analyze, and interpret the mind of Judaism appeals to the paramount status of a single, normative and norm-defining document, to which people turned for the details of how to conduct themselves, and which, in consequence, imparted not only information, but, through recurrent acts of consultation, a mode of thought as well. That single document, the Talmud of Babylonia or Bavli, so dominated the life of Jews in both Christian and Muslim civilizations that that writing formed the academy of the mind of Judaism. Therefore when we can characterize the mind conveyed within the pages of that writing, we may accurately assess the intellect of those whose lives found structure and sense there and nowhere else.

The specific question I answer is a very simple one of how Jewish intellects were so formed as to discern connections between one thing and something else and not other connections, and to draw one set of conclusions from the connections that are discerned rather than some other. Stated in more general terms, my proposition is that an explanation of mind matters because it tells us how an intellect common to a number of authoritative writings — hence, to a textual community — altogether makes sense of things. Modes of thought — intellects — transform information into knowledge, identify questions and answer them. People who think in a shared way moreover express their connections and conclusions to others, therefore they communicate and so form a community of sense, able to transact exchanges and accomplish shared discourse.

In this book, therefore, I tell the tale of the formation of the Jewish intellect from the beginning, with the writing of the Pentateuch in the fifth century B.C., to the climax, the definitive exemplification of that intellect in its final statement for late antiquity, with the closure of the Talmud of Babylonia or Bavli, in the sixth century A.D. I deal with two issues. First, I set forth those processes of thought that taught people to see things in one way and not in some other and consequently to say things in this way, not in that way. Second, I further propose to discern ways in which a later authorship within the ongoing Jewish intellectual formation situated itself in relationship to an earlier one. That is to say, I investigate the manner in which the results of thought were placed into the context of an ongoing and enduring realm of intellect. The first issue predominates in the earlier part of the book, the second in the later, as a tradition, beginning with the Pentateuchal Judaism, confronted later system-builders and demanded that they explain their work in relationship to a now-authoritative system. For, as we all recognize, systems turn into traditions and form a challenge and a burden to the system-builders of the future. That is the story of culture when a civilization retains its ties to a long-ago past, and, in a limited case, we shall see how, through an ingenious use of logic, one set of system-builders met the challenge of tradition by representing as a received tradition what was in fact their fresh and autonomous system, the statement they themselves put together and made up. We shall furthermore realize the originality of their accomplishment, the representation of a system as tradition, when we compare the counterpart problem facing Christian intellectuals, namely, the turning of traditions into a system. Then the two-sided dilemma facing the several heirs of the Hebrew Scriptures in Judaism and in Christianity becomes clear, and, with it, the two solutions that form the inheritance from the formative age for the intellectuals of the West from then to now. True, the subject seems somewhat off the main stream. But the issues turn out to be compelling and acutely contemporary whenever people address to a tradition the problems of the hour and place within the context of that tradition the system they work out for their own day.

For (to speak of the past, even though the problem is contemporary too) when a group of like-thinking intellectuals made its connections, drew its conclusions, in its rigorous thought the authorship made up its system and so, one way or another, wrote its book and accounted for the authority and context of the system expressed in that book. In the very process of thinking and framing its conclusions, that authorship faced the task of explaining how what it had thought and then said pertained to what other authorities had handed on in those prior writings that formed the inheritance of truth for the current mind. Thought proceeds always in a context, whether one of logic and process or proposition and proportion and composition. And context always is social. It follows that integral to the formation of the Jewish mind is an account of how by addressing others, that is, facing outward toward the social situation, the mind accounts for itself — process and proposition alike — in its context. These two questions then frame the inquiry at hand.

The Jewish intellect in classical times begins in ca. 500 B.C. and concludes its unfolding in ca. A.D. 600. That intellect comes to expression in the writings of Judaic authors first in Scripture, in particular, the Pentateuch, and infamy in the Talmud of Babylonia or Bavli. In-between a number of systemic statements emerged, of which the three that will engage our attention are those in the Essene library of Qumran and the Mishnah. We therefore consider the literary evidences for the structure of four intellects. At the end we briefly address the solution to the problem of holding together both a system and a set of inherited traditions that was worked out by those who created the Bible, that is, the Christian canon encompassing the Old and New Testaments. We shall see how they solved, in form, the counterpart issue: presenting traditions as a system. Then we gain perspective on the representation of a system as tradition that the authorship of the Bavli produced, and, in the comparison, we gain further insight on the comparison of the Judaic to the Christian intellect.

By "intellect" I mean in particular two traits among many that may characterize how people think. The first is how they connect one thing to something else, one fact to another, or, in literary terms, one sentence to another. When people find self-evident the relationship between one thing and another, we want to know why: the self-evidence of the obvious. Second come the ways in which they form the connections that they make into large-scale conclusions, encompassing statements, even entire systems of thought on the social order. Drawing conclusions from connections, people propose explanations for why things are one way, rather than some other. These two then go together to form a principal component of mind or intellect. For when we know how people are thinking, from the knowledge of the process of thought we also can describe propositions they are likely to reach. That is to say, how does the result of connection generate large-scale composition of ideas? These two stages — the perception of connection, the discernment of (to the engaged, the self-evidently valid) conclusions based on the connection — characterize mind or intellect, for they dictate how people think: in one way, rather than in some other. They further allow us to explore the potentialities and also the limitations of intellect, what people are likely to see one thing or to miss some other. But processes of thought lead us to the boundaries between mind and the systems that link mind to social reality. When processes of the organization of data and the interpretation of the result come to fruition, they yield a large-scale system, a view of the world, an account of how people are to conduct life, and a theory of the social entity that embodies that world-view and way of life.

That is why another critical issue in the formation, in ancient times, of the Jewish intellect carries us from the analysis of logic to the interpretation of structures of social meaning, statements of a well-proportioned and well-composed, systematic character that account not only for interior mentality but also for public meaning and conduct. Over eleven hundred years, diverse Jewish intellects set forth systems or structures, in which they put together their conceptions of this and that into a cogent and well-proportioned composition. The first of these accounts of (an) "Israel," the social entity, explaining the distinctive social character of that entity, describing its way of life, setting forth its view of the world, of course, was the Pentateuch, of ca. 500 B.C. The last was the Talmud of Babylonia or Bavli. Minds in-between confronted the same question, the one of the place and role of system-builders beyond the initial and original ones who stood behind the Pentateuch. Among all writers after the first generation in the ongoing context of Israel, the Jewish people, the issue of continuity proved paramount.

For the initial system, the Pentateuch, was set forth as God's revelation to Moses at Sinai, in consequence of which all subsequent authorships had to make their statements, set forth the social system for their "Israel," explaining its way of life and invoking its self-evidently valid world-view, in the shadow of that mountain. At the same time, these intellects erected what were in particular their structures, set forth their systems, put together their compositions. And that tension between the received and what each system-builder wished to give set forth a chronic, and occasionally acute, problem. For each writer in succession had to situate his writing in relationship to that authoritative one. That is to say, every author (or authorship) finds a place in a tradition or, alternatively, sets forth an independent and free-standing systemic statement of his own. As the latter sort of writing accumulated, the problem of tradition went from chronic to acute status and had to be worked out.

That yields two distinct points of analysis of the Jewish intellect, the one attending to the inner logic of cogent discourse, the other taking up the quite distinct issue of continuity and innovation. The story that I tell, therefore, is how the Jewish intellect took shape in two dimensions, the interior and the public. The analysis and classification of the logic of a systemic statement leads us into the inner workings of mind. The assessment and interpretation of the position defined by an authorship for itself in relationship to the received writings, or "tradition," instructs us on the shape and structure of the outer formation of that same mind. And the result of this second inquiry allows us to characterize and classify large-scale statements: are they traditional or systematic, historical or philosophical?

After the work of definition in Chapter Eight, I take up the categories of system as against tradition in Chapter Nine. If we can plausibly answer two questions, we shall know pretty much whatever we can discern about how the Jewish mind was formed and did its work: made connections and drew the conclusions that it reached, and, furthermore, set forth in plausible context of continuity, whether synchronic, whether diachronic, the consequent system of thought (where there was a system of thought) in its larger setting within the life of Israel's received system(s). The one question leads us to recognize how people determined that what they deemed self-evidently true was true. The other teaches us how they located truth within the continuum of an ongoing culture. Once, in Part One, I unpack these propositions of an analytical program, in Part Two, I survey important evidences of the Jewish intellect in the processes of formation. Then, in Part Three, I show how two distinct groups sorted out the problems of system and tradition. This they did by framing an encompassing structure to transmit, to a waiting world, that well-composed and staunchly constructed intellect that Jews (and, in their context, Christians too) would replicate in age succeeding age, hence the comparison of the Bavli to the Bible as two modes of making in a traditional context a systemic statement.

When I speak of intellect, I turn for my evidence to the writings that authorships produced. That points to what is the sole undemonstrated premise of this book. It is that the way in which people use language places on display the modes of thought that yield the connections and conclusions they propose. But that premise takes up a position on deep and solid foundations in Western philosophy, and I need not spell out what, in our context, the generality of learning now deems an established principle of inquiry. That is why I appeal to the syntax and grammar of writings in expounding the modes of thought that resort in particular to that syntax and grammar. My story narrates not the history of literature, first this book, then that book, but rather the tale of intellect and thought: the account of the stages of mindful analysis of how people made connections and drew conclusions.

What we say and the way in which we say it indicates how we think and the manner in which we frame hypotheses (make connections) and draw conclusions (test and evaluate and impute meaning or consequence to connections). I know no other data of a concrete order, available for analysis, than the workings of language in literature (oral or written, it makes no difference).

My fundamental premise, on which all else rests, therefore, is that intellect endures in language, modes of thought in syntax and sentence structure, which realize in concrete ways abstract processes of reasoning. The intellect reaches us only in its results, and, for the case of a set of systems that take form in writing, these results are the sentences formed into paragraphs, the paragraphs into chapters, the chapters into books: the truths deemed self-evidently valid, the propositions held beyond all debate, yielding the intense disagreement on this and that that serves as the wherewithal of everyday thought. The stakes in writing are higher still. For the books of a long-dead past live on and shape the everyday reality of Judaism today. One particular version of the Jewish intellect or mind exists in the here and now of decisions on what I should do and why I should do it, the meaning of things, the past and future, the hope and destination, the sense of the whole and the fittingness of each part. The stakes are very high.

If therefore we wish to understand what people think, we had best first ask how they think, and to know how people think, we analyze their writing: modes of making up sentences and joining them together into paragraphs, manner of composing paragraphs into chapters, chapters into books — all translated into the abstractions of knowledge, from fact to proposition, from proposition to encompassing theory. That means explaining the ways in which they choose the problems they find urgent, know that one set of data pertains and another does not. So we have to account for how the writers of authoritative documents make connections between this and that. All of these abstracts come to immediate and concrete expression not in sentences but in paragraphs, that is to say, in the composition of two or more sentences. These points of union, the joining of two facts into a proposition that transcends them both, the making of a whole that exceeds the sum of the parts — these acts of intellectual enchantment wonderfully form the smallest whole units of propositional thought. When, therefore, we know why this, not that, why a paragraph looks one way, rather than some other, we find ourselves at the very center of the working of a mind: its making of sense out of the nonsense presented by the detritus of mere information.

Now if we want to understand how the intellectuals of a social entity make sense of things, we examine the language they use in order to speak sensibly. That language presents the evidence on how people both reach and convey conclusions of consequence. When we can understand how people discern relationship between one fact, that is, one sentence, and another fact, or sentence, and further set forth conclusions to be drawn from the relationship or connection, we know not only what they think, but, from the character of the connection, how they think. So God lives in the syntax of cogent thought and intelligible statement of thought, and a Judaism is the statement of a process, yielding, of course, proposition as well. The propositions vary from document to document (though of course cogent all together), but the process, which characterizes all documents, uniformly imposes its connections and ubiquitously generates its conclusions.

Now let me explain one somewhat unfamiliar word-choice I have made. In examining the modes of thought of ultimately-canonical writings, when I show the range of choices, I call these modes of making connections and drawing conclusions "logics," meaning, specifically, the modes of intelligible discourse. Linking in a cogent way one sentence to another, one thought to another, these logics exhibited by the canonical writings of the diverse Judaisms of ancient times are many. We survey them all, to place into context the single one that predominated at the end of the protracted formative age of Judaism. I propose to show how, by thinking in one way rather than in some other, the framers of the Bavli solved the critical problem that faced any Judaism, and that will continue to confront anyone who proposes to participate in, but also to reshape, a historical tradition concerning religion and culture. I further relate the problem addressed by the authorship of the Bavli to the issue of identifying a canon and imputing to its contents cogency and systematic coherent. So the issues at hand are by no means parochial, and the results bear implications, and I hope, insight, for those trying to understand a variety of religious traditions, in particular, the species of religious traditions that claim to be both traditional and also systematic.

That is a dimension of interpretation I can only briefly outline here in my final chapter, in contrasting the Bible and the Bavli. For, over time, diverse Christianities would appeal for the context of discrete, systemic statements to the process and premise of canon, inclusive of creed. This canon, or Bible would construct the choice of systems to form an encompassing pattern of Christian truth. By contrast later Judaic systems or Judaisms would present as a single, seamless truth, an incremental tradition reaching back to Sinai, what were in fact sequential and distinct systems. So the one would impute the standing of a single system to remarkable varied traditions,. And, on the contrary, the other would adopt for its definitive document the status of tradition, alleging that what was in fact an orderly and elegantly composed system had simply accumulated. The outcome, in the modern age of the decay of both into the mentality of positivism, would produce mere facts, in the one world, facts of theology, and, in the other, facts of history, each a mode of making a statement that emptied of all force the intellects that endured in the power of words of the received writings.

CHAPTER EIGHT

THE FORMATION OF INTELLECT

My analysis of the intellect of Judaism addresses not only the how of thought, but also the what. For I want to know how a given mode of thought generated a given Judaic system, that is, a large-scale composition that draws many connections into a single coherent composition. Accordingly, in this book I claim to do two things.

First, in line with what has already been said in the first half of this book, I describe the mind or intellect displayed in Jewish writings in the formative age, over a period of more than a thousand years, from before the formation of the Pentateuch, in ca. 500 B.C., and other parts of the Hebrew Scriptures, through the Talmud of Babylonia or Bavli, in ca. A.D. 600, with a great many stops in-between, some of them at stations now deemed not Jewish of (in my terms) Judaic, but then understood as Jewish (Judaic). I specify the paramount processes of thought that dictated how people put two and two together and came out at four — connection, conclusion — as these processes are portrayed in concrete writings of the age and show how each comes to full and rich realization in some of those writings. That is what I mean by the formation of the mind of Judaism.

Second, I ask how intellects of Judaic systems that set forth those systems worked out the issue of their own relationship to minds that had gone before. That is, I ask about the relationship between system and tradition, the incremental growth of information and the organization of facts into purposeful statements of truths. I want to know how intellects addressed the issue of relating their ideas, their systems or statements, to received ideas and systems, that is, to what, to the moderns, was received as tradition. Some intellects worked in isolation from others. They made their statements essentially autonomously. These statements then reached the hands of others, who grouped various statements or documents and selected authoritative ones, declaring them canonical. In doing so, they formed of intellects a single mind, a canon of Christian truth, for example, called "the Bible." The task before heirs to this (as it happens, bifurcated) intellect became the discovery of the pattern of Christian truth, the identification of orthodoxy apart from heresy, for instance, as a literary-canonical exercise with its theological task. But other intellects solved the problem of received systems not by declaring them tradition, then defining a canon and imputing cogency to diverse writings in that canon. They did so, rather, by making the statement of their own system in the very heart of a received one. They formed a canon of truth, of revealed Torah, by inventing a logic of cogent discourse, that is, a set of ands (in the terms defined just now) that made connections in a way different from the logic of drawing conclusions, a set of equals, through which, as a matter of fact, their system reached its full and orderly statement.

Let us take up the first of the two questions, the one that concerns modes of thought. An ongoing social entity inculcates in age succeeding age modes of thought that, shared by all, set into context and impart self-evidence and enduring sense to otherwise discrete and transient propositions. These modes of thought, the processes of intellect, endure, even while the facts of the moment pass away. minds change on this and that. But intellect or mind does not. For modes of patterned thought on ephemera form of facts propositions, turning information into knowledge, knowledge into a system of explanation and therefore a shared structure of sensibility and meaning for the social order. And what mind does to begin with is tell people about interesting connections between one thing, one fact for instance, and some other, therefore instructing them on what deserves notice, and what can be ignored.

The simple sequence moves us from two unrelated facts to two connected facts and thence to a proposition or the drawing of a conclusions, so: [1] I threw a rock at a dog. It rained. [2] I threw a rock at a dog, then it rained. [3] If I throw a rock at a dog, it will rain. Some facts are inert, others bear consequence. Facts that fail to intersect with others in general gain slight notice; those that form structures and convey sense gain systematic consequence and ultimately form an encompassing account of how things are and should be, why we do things one way and now another: an ethos, an ethics, an account of a "we," altogether, a system. mind moreover explains to people about the consequences of the connections that they are taught to perceive, yielding conclusions of one sort, rather than another, based on one mode of drawing conclusions from the connections that are made, rather than some other. Accordingly, while the social entity undergoes change, processes endure to preserve the rules of deliberation that dictate the range of permissible deed. The realm of choice honors limits set by sense deemed common. What follows explains the urgency of the inquiry before us. How people think dictates the frontiers of possibility. The mind of Judaism, that is to say, process, is what defined, and will define, Judaisms in age succeeding age, so long as a Judaic system endures.

For the working or structure of "intellect" or "mind" in this book I use as a synonym a simple word, logic, but that is not in a technical sense. I mean the word "logic" to stand for the determinative principle of intelligibility of discourse and cogency of thought represented by stage [2] above. Logic that is shared among people makes possible the expression of thought in public discourse. And, for our study, logic is what tells people that one thing connects or intersects with another, while something else does not, hence, making connections; and logic further tells them what follows from the connections that they make, generating, as at stage [3] above, the conclusions that they are to draw. Accordingly, the first thing we want to know about any intellect, that is, in this context any piece of writing, is its logic of cogent discourse. Logic is what joins one sentence to the next and forms the whole into paragraphs of meaning, intelligible propositions, each with its place and sense in a still larger, accessible system. And logic as a matter of fact makes possible the sharing of propositions of general intelligibility and therefore forms the cement of a social system. For, because of logic, one mind connects to another, so that, in writing or in orally formulated and orally transmitted teaching, public discourse becomes possible. Because of logic debate on issues of general interest takes place. Still more to the point, because of logic a mere anthology of statements about a single subject becomes a composition of theorems about that subject, so that facts serve to demonstrate and convey propositions. Through logic the parts, bits and pieces of information, add up to a sum greater than themselves, generate information or insight beyond what they contain. What people think — exegesis of discrete facts in accord with a fixed hermeneutic of the intellect — knows no limit. How they think makes all the difference. In order to spell out the logic or principle of cogent discourse I therefore choose to focus upon the simple matter of the making connections and drawing conclusions from those connections.

Now when I claim to say how people make connections and draw conclusions, I seek substantiation of that claim in evidence of a concrete and immediately accessible character. This I find, in particular, in the way sentences cohere and make sense, the manner in which paragraphs gain cogency and set forth an intelligible statement. For that purpose, we turn survey the several answers an authorship gives to a simple question: how do one and one equal two? We want only to define the *and* and the *equal*, simple parts of speech, so to speak. Idioms lose currency, styles change, values and even concrete theological propositions shift in the passage of time. What is self-evidently true to one generation is true but merely trivial to another,

Rabbinic Judaism's Generative Logic: Volume Two

and urgent issues today retire into a merely chronic state, winning only desultory curiosity for themselves, in hardly half a generation. But the making of connections — that is what endures.

For the way in which people add up two and two to make four always requires the appeal to the and, and that is what endures, that and of the two and two equal four, and, too, the equal, which is to say, the conclusion yielded by the and. The logic lasts: the and of making connections, the equal of reaching conclusions. This endures: the certainty that X + Y are connected and generate conclusion Z, but that (for purposes of discussion here) the symbol # and the number 4 are not connected and therefore, set side by side, produce a mere nonsense-statement. The intellect of any Judaism flourishes in processes of thought and comes to expression in the premises of self-evidence, more lastingly and more certainly than in the propositions of conviction and confession. Whatever people propose to state should resort to a highly limited range of putting two and two together to equal four. In due course I shall survey some of the possibilities of answers to the question: how do two and two validate that and that stands between them, and why do two and two equal four: connection, conclusion.

Now what is at stake in the answers to the stated question? I hold that when we can describe the mind of a social entity through sorting out the rules governing the reaching of discrete and disparate conclusions, then we can claim to understand how the mind of a society of like-minded people is formed, those generative rules of culture and regulations of intellect that succeeding generations receive from infancy and transmit to an unknowable future. Attitudes shift. Values and beliefs change. One generation's immutable truths come to the coming age as banalities or nonsense. But processes of reflection about the sense of things, modes of thought concerning how we identify and solve problems, above all, the making of connections between this and that — these endure like oceans and mountains. Shifting only in tides and currents so vast as to defy the grasp of time, so that, when they do quake, the whole earth moves, these processes and modes of mind in the end dictate structure and establish order, the foundations of all social life, the framework of all culture.

My fundamental argument is that the intellect in any given social setting and cultural context works in a particular way. Specifically, the mind forms propositions, which I just now referred to as putting two and two together to equal four. The italicized words *and* (standing for connections people make) and *equal* (representing conclusions people draw from those connections) form the hinge on which all else turns. When, moreover, we can explain a particular mode of joining these propositions together into sizable compositions of thought, we may ask questions about how intellects bring to consciousness and expression the work that they do: thought thinking about itself, so to speak. This they do by establishing a relationship between their thought and the results of the thought of prior authorships. Or they may do so by their (superficial) silence, pretense that they alone set forth a system, a judgment, a position, an argument, on an urgent question. In that case, they do not lay claim to participation in any context; their system is their own, free-standing statement. Between these two positions I see no alternative, but within the discipline of either one of them there are many ways to negotiate the logic and implications, as we shall see.

At the outset, therefore, it suffices to note only that in the interior working and structure of intellect I see two critical steps. The first is putting things together and drawing conclusions from them, which dictates how the mind works, the one, the and, the other, the equal. The second is defining the context for the upshot of intellect, defining one's place in, or in relationship to, a canon of truth or revelation. The former involves the presentation of a cogent and systematic statement. The latter, for instance, may impose the task of placing a system, a philosophical coherence, into a tradition, a historical happenstance. Or it may require others to find the shared and harmonious truth inherent in a variety of systematic statements, to impose canonical standing and to demonstrate coherent composition among many such statements. In that case a system is received within a larger theological or philosophical composition or construction. In so stating, I have moved beyond the problem at hand, which is one of defining, to begin with, what we mean by intellect, the working of the *and* and the *equal.* But not to estimate the power of that equal, and its dimensions! For in the end, the force of the "equal" is such as to make the whole of the social world, the statement, in the end, of that inner logic of intellect that holds together, by imparting self-evident truth to, the entirety of the social order. We shall return to that consideration in the next chapter. Let us attend, rather, to how we answer the question at hand.

Precisely what evidence tells us about the *and* and the *equal?* It is the evidence of the written word. Let me expand on this point, since it makes possible the argument of the entire book. The "intellect," or "mind," is formed by modes of thought and expression through which people discern connections between different things and draw conclusions. When people convey to others the connections that they make and the conclusions that they reach, they do so in a way intelligible to the social entity of which they are a part. From the manner of public discourse or expression of thought, we work our way back to the intellect or mind that is represented by words made into intelligible sentences and by sentences that form paragraphs and set forth propositions. For the mode of thought is realized in the connection and conclusion stated in words. When, therefore, we know how people make connections and draw conclusions, we know — so I claim — whatever we shall ever understand about their intellect and how it works. That is why I claim to be able to describe the formation of the mind of Judaism from the Hebrew Bible through the Bavli.

When we see how people put their thoughts together in writing, we get whatever factual knowledge we are going to have about how they make connections and draw conclusions from those connections. The very means by which these modes of thought were transmitted and held together, the extraordinary power of analysis and argument characteristic of the normative documents — these then come to us from the writings of a social group, each pertinent to its cultural context, all of them — by definition — examples of what some, within that group, identified as possibilities. And the mind sorts out an infinity of possibilities in reaching its decisions about what fits together with what else, and what difference the fit makes: making connections, drawing conclusions, the *and* and the *equal.*

This brings us to the second of the two questions with which I began, namely, the way in which intellects related their connections and conclusions to the upshot of connections and conclusions reached by prior minds — is critical to what I propose to accomplish, which is the explanation of how the mind of Judaism worked from the formation of its initial documents to the closure of its definitive writing. And to me that means not only the logic of cogent discourse. It also means the consciousness of the context in which discourse takes place. I mean to address the issue, in concrete terms to be sure, of thought thinking about itself, so to speak.

Let me expand on this point, which forms the true generative problematic here. I am struck by the problem confronting all Judaic thinkers, including system-builders, from the formation of the Pentateuch. It concerned the relationship of their systems to the original system become tradition, that is, the Pentateuch itself. From Scripture onward, Judaic system-builders thought through not only the cogent world-view, way of life, and definition of the social entity that they proposed to set before the "Israel" of their own invention. They also linked their systems to (one or some or, by reason of stunning independence of mind, none of) those that had gone before, and so claimed to think within a tradition of revelation and thought. Or they claimed an autonomy of mind that permitted them to state what they conceived to be revelation within the fresh setting of their own original thought. I want, therefore, to explain not only how Jews made connections and drew conclusions. I propose also to account for how intellectuals set forth the coherent systems they worked out and, in writing, presented to their "Israel."

These two issues — logic of discourse, consciousness of the context of thought — seem to me inseparable. For as soon as minds become conscious of thought, they have also to uncover their own relationship to the thought of others, before and in their own time, and, further, dictate what they wished to have as their relationship to those who would come afterward. Some intellects set forth their thought, in a whole system, out of all relationship to all other thought. But one authorship, that is, one cogent group of thinkers, laid out a systemic statement in which, drawing conclusions within one logic, making connections within a different logic, they took account of the critical issue of history and society in the life of intellect. Relating themselves to all that had gone before, that is, taking up a position within a tradition, that set of intellectuals also put forth a stunningly coherent system of its own.

What is at stake in this account becomes clear only at the end of our inquiry. It turns out to be the uniqueness, in its context, of the mind of Judaism in one particular document, what turned out to be the most important one of all time. The mind of Judaism of the Bavli, which, I shall show, had no counterpart, made the mind of Jewry from its time to our own. That mode of thought that the Bavli set forth, making connections in a conventional way, but drawing conclusions in a most unusual way, in fact solved a vast problem of cogent thought in a traditional system that had been left open for the antecedent millennium. The authorship of the Bavli both set forth its own strikingly coherent system and also presented that system in such a way as to impute to it origin within the incremental process of received truth from Sinai, that is to say, as tradition. In demonstrating the Bavli's unprecedented solution to the problem of both receiving truth and also independently making connections and drawing conclusions, a problem facing the intellect of Judaism from scriptural times forward, I account for how Jews for the fourteen centuries after the Bavli made connections and drew conclusions.

So while I speak only of the formative age, from the Hebrew Bible through the Talmud of Babylonia, in fact I describe the formation of the mind of Judaism for so long as there was a single, cogent mind of Judaism, which is, for nearly all time. The simple fact is that for many centuries down to our own day we could confidently claim to describe a mind that was distinctively and particularly Jewish. It was (and for many, still is) a mind trained to work in one way, not in some other, to make connections and to draw conclusions in accord with a particular protocol of cogency and logic. That mind was born and shaped in the Bavli. In the long progress from Scripture, in particular the Pentateuch, which came to closure, it is generally agreed, at ca. 500 B.C. (some time after the destruction of the first temple of Jerusalem in 586 B.C. and before the arrival of Nehemiah and Ezra to supervise the rebuilding of the second in ca. 450 B.C.), to the conclusion of the Bavli, in ca. A.D. 600, there was a broad variety of mind of Judaisms. Most of them found a parallel in modes of thought of other kinds of writings, deriving from non-Jews. Point for point, we can find in the modes of making connections and drawing conclusions in Jewish writings counterparts in gentile ones, whether Greek and Roman or Christian. But at the end, one mode of cogent discourse emerged, which, so far as I know, characterizes only Jewish writing, and therefore also, only Jewish thinking. That is the mode of cogent discourse realized in the Bavli. When we trace what was common and what proved distinctive to Jewish writing, therefore, we see one reason for the power of the Bavli to make, and also make up, the mind of Judaism from the time of its closure to nearly our own day. Not knowing all the possibilities of identifying connections and reaching conclusions, I cannot allege, and do not even imagine, that the Bavli is unique among the written representations of mind that humanity has put forth. But I do claim that, in the writing of the West in its formative age, and even to our own day, there is simply nothing quite like it, and, it must follow, minds made in the model of the Bavli will bear an extraordinary shape and irreplicable imprint.

Accordingly, each mode of thought spun out over more than a thousand years dictated the way in which a given kind of writing would be composed: what sorts of things were found coherent with one another, which ways of putting things together proved self-evidently valid. But at the end came one mode of thought, that is, making connections, drawing conclusions — and placing those conclusions on exhibit for others to examine and confront, and that made all the difference from then to nearly the present day. That mode of thought came along to solve a problem of thought and culture, and it did solve that problem, as I shall explain. Specifically, the Bavli's mode of thought mediated between traditional and systematic or philosophical thought, finding a way to hold the two quite distinct modes of inquiry in balance. In tracing the path of the mind of Judaism from Scripture, through every sort of Jewish writing, upward to the Bavli, I tell the story of the formation of the mind of Judaism that, from the Bavli to the contemporary world, worked in its distinctive way, for its particular purposes, to draw its own conclusions, whatever they might be.

Let me now also state what I do not propose to accomplish here. What are not at stake in this book are issues of sociology or cultural anthropology. I claim to describe the interiority of the intellect, to account only for the shape and structure of mind in the circumstance of what was admittedly a socially-facing system. I do not address Jews' culture throughout time or even in antiquity alone. I do not claim that all, or most, or at least all "authentic," Jews think, characteristically, in one way and not in some other. I do not even claim to know how the people who made the Pentateuch, or the Essene library of Qumran, or the Mishnah, or the Bavli, thought in general. I only allege that I know how, in the writing of theirs that we do have, they made connections and drew conclusions, and, further, I claim also to know how (if at all) they related their writing and the system it presented to prior ones. The evidence lies at hand: the documents themselves. I describe on the basis of concrete statements in their language and order and composition and set forth for their purposes not how people were but how some people thought, the imagination of a few concerning the affairs of the many. If made as a statement of either negative evaluation or self-praise, an account of the intellect of Judaism would form an expression of mere racism or ethnic aggrandizement, therefore one of no-account romanticism. If made as an allegation of fact, that would constitute a statement of sociology or of cultural anthropology, not one of the logic of connection, such as I wish to make. Pertinent evidence for those fields derives not only from the and that joins sentences or the equal that forms of sentences a syllogism. Other facts intervene.

More to the point, I know no studies that sustain the claim that there is a distinctively "Jewish" way of thought, characteristic of all Jews and no gentiles. But there were religious systems, Judaisms, each with its own rules of intellect and conduct, its integrity, its definitive (and therefore, to itself) unique traits. And in the canonical writings of those Judaisms I can show that there was, and is, a distinctively (but none can claim, uniquely) a intellect of Judaism, or a Judaic mode of thought. For, as I shall demonstrate, as a matter of description of the logic of connection, the canonical writings of the several Judaisms of ancient times, from the Pentateuchal one onward, do reach and express conclusions in one way and not in some other, and I therefore can provide an account of the making of the mind of not the Jews but Judaism: the canonical writings, seen whole and complete, that constitute the statement of Judaism, its world-view, way of life, and address to the social entity, "Israel," of its invention.

I of course do not allege that the principal repertoire of logics characteristic of the several canonical authorships, respectively, is distinctive to that canon, for that is something I cannot show and therefore do not know. I do find remarkable the mixture of logics characteristic of the Bavli, but even that is not unique to that authorship. I suspect that we may point to other religious systems that appeal for cogency and order to those same principles that operate in Judaism. I allege only that people who form the authorships of the writings we examine did make choices and did determine in one way and not in some other to form their cogent statements of connection, to draw conclusion from discerned connection. What is characteristic of a group of writings tells us how those writers thought, and I claim to describe that mode of thought without alleging no other group of writers thought that way, let alone that all writers within Judaism from then to now thought that way and no other way. Describing traits characteristic of one set of writings requires showing only that people made choices, not that their choices were unique to them.

Still, as a matter of fact, I tend to think that the Bavli forms an instrument of cultural expression and continuity without significant parallel in the history of the literate cultures of humanity — though each, self-evidently, has had its equivalent to the Bavli. But comparisons of a global nature lie far beyond the distant horizons of this exercise, even though, I do believe, the time will come, also, for comparison, even of considerable dimensions indeed. And, as I said at the outset, the two other formative and definitive traits of the world we know, capitalism and democracy, also emerged within religious worlds other than the Judaic one, and that too requires explanation. But not here, not now, and not necessarily by me. Now to the task at hand, beginning with the explanation of why I identify as "mind" or "intellect" the work of making connections and drawing conclusions.

It follows that the intellect of Judaism is formed by people who see connections and therefore draw conclusions — and write books to share them with their imagined "Israel." They form Judaisms, that is, coherent statements of a world-view and a way of life addressed to a specified social entity called an "Israel." Intellectuals, after all, are the unacknowledged legislators of all realms of human action in society, and, it goes without saying, intellect of Judaisms form Judaisms. When, therefore, we know how that intellect works, we understand the processes that yield Judaisms. We in the contemporary West readily understand what is at stake in the formation of the shared and social intellect of an entire community of mind; it is the discovery of knowledge we today call scientific or philosophical. The mind of Judaism, like Western science and the great tradition of philosophy, undertook the quest for "unity underlying apparent diversity, simplicity underling apparent complexity, order underlying apparent disorder, regularity underlying apparent anomaly." The quest for order and (therefore also) explanation required the making of connections between one thing and something else and the drawing of conclusions from those discerned connections. All together, the answers to the question of how people make connections and draw conclusions tell us the processes of thought. What of the claim thereby also to know the intellect of Judaism? What I mean is very simple. I refer to what is called a textual community. Let me explain.

The matter of process grasped, we know how the mind of that social entity frames the propositions that it proposes as its system and the foundation of its order. Accordingly, by definition the logic of intelligible discourse, the premise of self-evident comprehension, above all, the intangible sensibility that makes connections between one thing and something else and yields conclusions transcending them both — these are what hold together many minds in one community of shared and mutually intelligible speech that, in the aggregate, we may call society, in our instance, the society of a Judaism or of the "Israel" at hand. The evidence for that shared intellect, that mind in common, therefore comes to us in how people speak to one another, in the connections each makes between two or more sentences and in the connections all make with one another. The formation of a shared intellect, the making of a mind in common — these derive from process and connection. This book aims to describe the making of the mind of Judaism, by which I mean, the ways in which authorships of the formative canonical writings of Judaism defined connections between one sentence and another and drew conclusions from those connections, the public logic of common and (perceivedly) cogent discourse.

From the language people used to say to one another what they were thinking, I therefore propose to move backward to the processes of thought encapsulated in that language. If people state a proposition, I want to know the argumentation in behalf of that proposition, the kind of evidence and the manner of marshalling that evidence, and why they took for granted other people would find it all persuasive. Still more to the point, if people see a connection, I want to ask what makes the connection self-evident to them, so that one thing fits with some other, and another thing does not. For the mind of Judaism is not abstract , and the Judaism that that mind defines does not deal solely in abstractions. The authors of the canonical writings of the Judaism of the formative age mastered the requirements of applied reason and practical logic. But that means they also were masters of intellect and logical acumen. Consequently, we have in hand ample evidence, in concrete terms, of both the decisions people reached, the ways in which they framed their propositions, and also, the expectation that others within the group educated in their writings and manners of thought would find the result compelling. That is why I claim the mind of a Judaism finds ample documen-

Rabbinic Judaism's Generative Logic: Volume Two 15

tation in the writings of that Judaism. And — so I maintain — we may reconstruct how people think from what they say. And because, for long centuries, all Judaists read the same books and communicated within the patterns of thought inculcated by those books, we may speak not only of the mind of Judaism but also the textual community that embodied and realized that mind.

The bridge from proposition, that is, what people think, to process, how they think, therefore is built of modes of discourse preserved and transmitted in writing: mutually intelligible exchanges of ideas, in fully articulated language made up of words and sentences that follow a public syntax. Discourse thus refers to the way in which people make their statements so that the connections within their thought are intelligible and cogent to others (and that by definition, hence the stress on the public). To describe the modes of discourse which attest to modes of thought at the deep structure of mind, we ask how people place on display not only the conclusions they have reached but also the manner in which they wish to announce and argue in favor of those conclusions — all together, the way in which they make their statement of their position. Accordingly, it is in cogent argument concerning proposition that mind becomes incarnate.

That is why I work my way back from the way in which people compose their cogent and persuasive statements to the mind, the intellect, that teaches them not only or mainly what to think, but rather, how to think. My claim, now fully set forth, is that the intellect, an abstraction, finds form in a fully-exposed manner of reaching and demonstrating a particular statement of sense. That intellect or mind takes place, for instance, in the framing of a proposition, complete in exposition, from beginning statement through middle demonstration and argumentation to end conclusion and the drawing of consequences. For mind cannot endure in abstract theory, contemplating itself alone, but has its work to do. And not only so, but mind or intellect also flourishes in society, and that means, within a tradition of thought and a context of ongoing process. These two then, logic of cogent discourse, characteristic of mind, and tradition of thinking, definitive of the context of mind, combine in the process that yields systemic construction and composition. And the task of intellect is always and everywhere both to think afresh but also to state the results within the setting of the society that is meant to receive and embody the consequent system of intellect. Through a considerable argument, we shall now see that the two work together, logic and system, to produce order and structure, and that the textual community has then to place into enduring cultural and social context the order and structure of the hour. When we know how a Judaic system not only did its work but also established its place in an ongoing labor of culture, we shall understand the mind of Judaism.

PART ONE

TWO ISSUES
IN THE ANALYSIS OF THE JEWISH INTELLECT

CHAPTER NINE

THE MODALITY OF INTELLECT:
SYSTEMATIC OR TRADITIONAL?

The life of intellect may commence morning by morning. Or it may flow from an ongoing process of thought, in which one day begins where yesterday left off, and one generation takes up the task left to it by its predecessors. A system by definition starts fresh, defines first principles, augments and elaborates them in balance, proportion, above all, logical order. In a traditional process, we never start fresh but only add, to an ongoing increment of knowledge, doctrine, and mode of making judgment, our own deposit as well. And, in the nature of such an ongoing process, we never start fresh, but always pick and choose, in a received program, the spot we choose to augment. The former process, the systematic one, begins from the beginning and works in an orderly, measured and proportioned way to produce a cogent, and neatly composed statement, a philosophy for instance. Tradition by its nature is supposed to describe not a system, whole and complete, but a process of elaboration of a given, received truth: exegesis, not fresh composition. And, in the nature of thought, what begins in the middle is unlikely to yield order and system and structure laid forth ab initio. In general terms, systematic thought is philosophical in its mode of analysis and explanation, and traditional thought is historical in its manner of drawing conclusions and providing explanations.

In terms of the two logics that we found to form cogent discourse, the one is philosophical, generates well-crafted propositions, puts them together into a whole that holds together neatly all of the parts, and in method and literary form syllogistic, the other is teleological and, at its foundations, in method and literary form narrative: first this, then that, therefore this comes prior to that. And, I should claim, system and tradition not only describe incompatible modes of thought but also generate results that cannot be made to cohere. For the conflict between tradition and system requires us to choose one mode of thought about one set of issues and to reject the other mode of thought and also the things about which thought concerns itself. And that choice bears profound consequences for the shape of mind.

So far as "tradition" refers to the matter of process, it invokes, specifically, an incremental and linear process that step by step transmits out of the past statements and wordings that bear authority and are subject to study, refinement, preservation, and transmission. In such a traditional process, by definition, no one starts afresh to think things through. Each participant in the social life of intellect makes an episodic and ad hoc contribution to an agglutinative process, yielding, over time, (to continue the geological metaphor) a sedimentary deposit. The opposite process we may call systematic, in that, starting as if from the very beginning and working out the fundamental principles of things, the intellect, unbound by received perspectives and propositions, constructs a free-standing and well-proportioned system. In terms of architect the difference is between a city that just grows and one that is planned; a scrapbook and a fresh composition; a composite commentary and a work of philosophical exposition.

The one thing a traditional thinker knows is that he or she stands in a long process of thought, with the sole task of refining and defending received truth. And the systematic thinker affirms the task of starting fresh, seeing things all together, all at once, in the right order and proportion, a composition, not merely a composite, held together by an encompassing logic. A tradition requires exegesis, a system, exposition. A tradition demands the labor of harmonization and elaboration of the given. A system begins with its harmonies in order and requires not elaboration but merely a repetition, in one detail after another, of its main systemic message. A tradition does not repeat but only renews received truth; a system always repeats because it is by definition encompassing, everywhere saying one thing, which, by definition, is always new. A system in its own terms has no history; a tradition defines itself through the authenticity of its history.

Now there can be no doubt that, from the Bavli onward, the intellect of Judaism flowed along traditional lines, making its contribution, from generation to generation, as commentary, not fresh composition. Every available history of Jewish thought, academic and vulgar alike, represents the principal modality of intellect as the refinement, adaptation, or adjustment of a received increment of truth. However new and lacking all precedent, Judaic systems find representation as elaboration of received Torah, imputed to verses of Scripture, and not as a sequence of fresh and original beginnings of systematic and orderly statements of well-composed and cogent principles. As between the fresh and perfect classicism of the well-proportioned Parthenon and the confused and disorderly alleyways of the streets below, the intellect of Judaism made its residence in the side-alleys of the here and now, in an ongoing, therefore by definition never-neatly-constructed piazza.

The intellect of Judaism carried on its work through receiving and handing on, not through thinking through in a fresh and fundamental way, the inheritance of the ages. It sought to preserve the sediment of truth and add its layer, not to dig down to foundations and build afresh, even bound to using the dirt removed in the digging. But is that how things were in the classical age, from the formation of the Pentateuch to the closure of the Bavli? That is to say, was the intellect of Judaism in that formative age fundamentally traditional and historical, or essentially systematic and philosophical? At stake in the answer to that question is our fundamental characterization of the intellect of Judaism , in its successive writings, in ancient times.

We shall know the answer in two ways, formal and conceptual. The first, the merely formal, of course is the simpler. When an authorship extensively cites received documents and makes its statement through citing or clearly alluding to statements in those documents, then, on the face of it, that authorship wishes to present its ideas as traditional. It claims through its chosen form of expression (merely) to continue, (only) to amplify, extend, apply truth received, not to present truth discovered and demonstrated. That authorship then proposes to present its ideas as incremental, secondary, merely applications of available words. Not only so, but that authorship always situates itself in relationship to a received document, in the case of all Judaisms, of course, in relationship to the Pentateuch.

The second indicator, the conceptual, is the more subtle but also the more telling. When an authorship takes over from prior documents the problem and program worked out by those documents, contributing secondary improvements to an established structure of thought, then we may confidently identify that authorship as derivative and traditional. We realize that that is how matters were represented, in theory at least, by the framers of The Fathers, the opening statement of which is: "Moses received Torah at Sinai and handed it on to Joshua." Then a piece of writing stands in a chain of handing on and receiving, handing on and receiving, in the context of a Judaism, of course, from Sinai.

This brings us to the indicators of system as against tradition. A systematic, and by nature, philosophical, statement or document, by contrast, presents its ideas as though they began with its author or authorship, rather than alluding to, let alone citing in a persistent way, a prior writing, e.g., Scripture. The form of a systematic statement ordinarily will be autonomous. The order of discourse will begin from first principles and build upon them. The presentation of a system may, to be sure, absorb within itself a given document, citing its materials here and there. But — and this forms the indicator as to conception, not form alone — the authorship in such a case imposes its program and its problem upon received materials, without the pretense that the program and order of those inherited ("traditional" "authoritative" "scriptures") has made any impact whatsoever upon its presentation. An instance of a systematic statement's use of received materials is Matthew Chapter Two, which wishes to make the point that the events in the early years of Jesus fulfilled the promises of prophecy. That point requires the authorship to cite various verses; these are, of course, chosen for the occasion, and there is no pretense at a reading of whole passages in their "own" terms and in accord with their "own" momentum of meaning. The Matthean authorship, rather, makes its point, which is part of its larger program and polemic, through an incidental, if important, allusion to prophecy.

The basic criterion of the systematic character of a document or statement, however, derives from a quite distinct trait. It is the authorship's purpose and whether, and how, a statement serves that purpose. How do we know that a statement, a sizable composition for instance, is meant to be systematic? In a well-composed system, every detail will bear the burden of the message of the system as a whole. Each component will make, in its terms, the statement that the system as a whole is intended to deliver. In order to understand that fact, we have to appreciate an important distinction in the analysis of systems. It is between a fact that is systemically vital, and one that is inert. For the study of economics, this point has been made by Joseph A. Schumpeter as follows: "In economics as elsewhere, most statements of fundamental facts acquire importance only by the superstructures they are made to bear and are commonplace in the absence of such superstructures."

That is to say, a system of religious thought, comprising a world-view, a way of life, and a definition of the social entity meant to adopt the one and embody the other, makes ample use of available facts. In order to make their statement, the authors of the documents of such a system speak in a language common to their age. Some of these facts form part of the background of discourse, like the laws of gravity. They are, if important, inert, because they bear no portion of the burden of the systemic message. I call such facts inert. Other of these facts form centerpieces of the system; they may or may not derive from the common background. Their importance to the system forms part of the statement and testimony of that system.

Now in a well-composed system, every systemically generative fact will bear in its detail the message of the system as a whole, and, of course, inert facts will not. What I mean is simply illustrated. It is clear to any reader of Plato's Republic, Aristotle's Politics (and related corpus, to be sure), the Mishnah, or Matthew's Gospel, that these writers propose to set forth a complete account of the principle or basic truth concerning their subject, beginning, middle, and end. Accordingly, they so frame the details that the main point is repeated throughout. At each point in the composition, the message as a whole, in general terms, will be framed in all due particularity. The choices of topics will be dictated by the requirements of that prevailing systemic attitude and statement. We can even account, ideally, for the topical components of the program, explaining (in theory at least) why one topic is included and another not. A topic will find its place in the system because only through what is said about that particular topic the system can make the statement it wishes to make. Silence on a topic requires explanation, as much as we must supply a systemic motive or reason for the selection of, and substantial disquisition on, some other topic.

Our criterion for whether a document is traditional or systematic, therefore systemic, therefore allows us to test our judgment by appeal to facts of verification or falsification. For the importance of recognizing the systemically generative facts is simple. When we can account for both inclusion and exclusion, we know not merely the topical program of the system but its fundamental intent and method, and we may assess the system-builders success in realizing their program. A well-composed system will allow us to explain what is present and what is absent, as I said. Consequently, we may come to a reasonable estimation of the system's coverage, its realization of its program and full, exhaustive, presentation of its encompassing statement. Not only so, but a well-crafted systemic statement will by definition form a closed system, and the criterion of whether or not a statement stands on its own or depends upon other sources, e.g., information not contained within its encompassing statement but only alluded to by that statement, serves a second major indicator for taxonomic purposes. Let me spell this out.

Some systems say precisely what they want on exactly those topics that make it possible to make its full statement. These are what we may call "closed systems," in that the authors tell us — by definition — everything that they want us to know, and — again, by definition — nothing that they do not think we need to know. They furthermore do not as a matter of systemic exposition have to refer us to any other writing for a further explication of their meaning (even though for reasons of argument or apologetic, they may do so). When an authorship sets forth a topic and completely and exhaustively expounds that topic, it has given us a systematic statement. The authorship has laid out its program, described the structure of its thought, given us what we need to know to grasp the composition and proportion of the whole, and, of course, supplied the information that, in detail, conveys to us the statement in complete and exhaustive form, thus, a closed system. It has done more than simply add a detail to available information. Quite to the contrary, the authorship of a statement of a closed system will frame its statement in the supposition that that authorship will tell us not only what we need to know, but everything we need to know, about a given topic. And that is a solid indicator of a systematic statement. An open system, by contrast, requires the recipient of a statement to refer not only to what an authorship tells us, but also to what an authorship invokes. The program is partial, the statement truncated, the system incomplete and not in correct composition and proportion, if, indeed, there is a system at all. That will then mark a traditional, not a systemic, statement. A piece of writing that depends upon other writings, and that not occasioned by subjective judgment of the reader but by objective, if implicit, direction of the author, then forms part of an open system, or is not a systematic statement at all, but a fragment of thought.

Now in all that I have said, I have treated as an axiom the

formal and putative autonomy of systemic thought:, which is so represented as if it begins de novo every morning, in the mind, imagination, and also conscience, of the system-builders. But what of what has gone before: other systems and their literary, as well as their social, detritus? Let us turn to the relationships to prior writings exhibited by systematic and traditional authorships, respectively. How do we know the difference between a system and a tradition in respect to the reception of received systems and their writings? The criteria of difference are characterized very simply. A systematic authorship will establish connections to received writings, always preserving its own autonomy of perspective. A traditional authorship will stand in a relationship of continuity, commonly formal, but always substantive and subordinate, with prior writings. The authorship of a document that stands in a relationship of connection to prior writings will make use of their materials essentially in its own way. The authorship of a document that works in essential continuity with prior writings will cite and quote and refine those received writings but will ordinarily not undertake a fundamentally original statement of its own framed in terms of its own and on a set of issues defined separately from the received writings or formulations. The appeal of a systematic authorship is to the ineluctable verity of well-applied logic, practical reason tested and retested against the facts, whether deriving from prior authorities, or emerging from examples and decisions of leading contemporary authorities.

A traditional authorship accordingly will propose to obliterate lines between one document and another. A systematic authorship in the form of its writing ordinarily will not merge with prior documents. It cites the received writing as a distinct statement — a document out there — and does not merely allude to it as part of an internally cogent statement — a formulation of matters "in here." The systematic authorship begins by stating its interpretation of a received writing in words made up essentially independent of that writing, for example, different in language, formulation, syntax, and substance alike. The marks of independent, post facto, autonomous interpretation are always vividly imprinted upon the systematic authorship's encounter with an inherited document. Such a writing never appears to be represented by internal evidence as the extension of the text, in formal terms the uncovering of the connective network of relations, as literature a part of the continuous revelation of the text itself, in its material condition as we know it "at bottom, another aspect of the text." Not only so, but a systematic statement will not undertake the sustained imitation of prior texts by earlier ones. And even when, in our coming survey, we find evidence that, superficially, points toward a traditional relationship between and among certain texts that present us with closed systems and completed, systematic statements, we should, indeed, be struck by the independence of mind and the originality of authorships that pretend to receive and transmit, but in fact imagine and invent.

We shall now see as a trait of the mind of Judaism from the Pentateuchal statement to the Bavli, paramount and definitive indicators of originality in every document. We shall uncover few marks of imitation, but a vast corpus of indications of total independence, one document from the other, and thus an imputed claim of essential originality. Only one document will set forth, in form at least, a claim intrinsic to the presentation of its ideas that it constitutes a traditional, and not a systematic, statement, and that is the Bavli. And yet, we shall also see, the Bavli constitutes the most systematic statement of them all. How to account for the contradiction between the document's traditional form and philosophical, systematic composition? The question brings us, by a remarkably circuitous route, back to the matter of the logics of cogent discourse. For, as I shall try to show in the next part, which forms the shank of this book, that it is through the use of one logic, rather than another, that each document makes its autonomous and always-systematic statement. And that use of only a single logic of discourse left unsolved the problem of relating one's writing to others that had gone before, that is, to demonstrate the traditionality of what was, in fact, an autonomous presentation of a closed system. For if I had to specify a single aesthetic tension confronting any of our authorships, it is to establish a claim of continuity while doing pretty much anything someone wanted to do.

Accordingly, we proceed to further indicators of system as against tradition in the classification of writings and the minds that produced them. A traditional document (therefore the mind it represents) recapitulates the inherited texts; that defines the traditionality of such a writing. A systematic writing may allude to, or draw upon, received texts, but does not recapitulate them, except for its own purposes and within its idiom of thought. Traits of order, cogency, and unity derive from modes of thought and cannot be imposed upon an intellect that is, intrinsically, subordinated to received truth. A traditional writing refers back to, goes over the given. The system for its part not only does not recapitulate its texts, it selects and orders them, imputes to them as a whole cogency that their original authorships have not expressed in and through the parts, expresses through them its deepest logic. The system — the final and complete statement —does not recapitulate the extant texts. The antecedent texts — when used at all — are so read as to recapitulate the system. The system comes before the texts and so in due course defines the canon. But in introducing the notion of canon, I have moved far beyond my story. At this point it suffices to claim that the thought-processes of tradition and those of system-building scarcely cohere. Where applied reason prevails, the one — tradition — feeds the other — the system — materials for sustained reconstruction.

The statement of a system is worked out according to the choices dictated by that authorship's sense of order and proportion, priority and importance, and it is generated by the problematic found by that authorship to be acute and urgent and compelling. When confronting the task of exegesis of a received writing, the authorship of a systematic statement does not continue and complete the work of antecedent writings within a single line of continuity ("tradition"). Quite to the contrary, that authorship makes its statement essentially independent of its counterpart and earlier document. In a systematic writing, therefore, the system comes first. The logic and principles of orderly inquiry take precedence over the preservation and repetition of received materials, however holy. The mode of thought defined, the work of applied reason and practical rationality may get underway.

First in place is the system that the authorship through its considered, proportioned statement as a whole expresses and serves in stupefying detail to define. Only then comes that selection, out of the received materials of the past, of topics and even concrete judgments, facts that serve the system's authorship in the articulation of its system. Nothing out of the past can be shown to have dictated the systematic program, which is essentially the work of its authorship. The tradition is ongoing, and that by definition. Then, also by definition, the system begins exactly where and when it ends. Where reason reigns, its inexorable logic and order, proportion and syllogistic reasoning govern supreme and alone, revising the received materials and restating into a compelling statement, in reason's own encompassing, powerful and rigorous logic, the entirety of the prior heritage of information and thought.

Let me now conclude this protracted theoretical statement of the analysis now to follow. We shall now see in three of the four the cases subject to review here that the intellect of Judaism , from the Pentateuch to the Bavli, presented not stages or chapters in an unfolding tradition but closed systems, each one of them constituting a statement at the end of a sustained process of rigorous thought and logical inquiry, applied logic and practical reason. The only way to read a reasoned and systematic statement of a system is defined by the rules of general intelligibility, the laws of reasoned and syllogistic discourse about rules and principles. And the correct logic for a systematic statement is philosophical and propositional, whether syllogistic or teleological. Readers may now test whether my characterization of the prevailing logic and the correct classification of documents — propositional and systematic, or non-syllogistic and traditional — applies to important examples of the intellect of Judaism in the classical age. For consider the alternative. The way to read a traditional and sedimentary document by contrast lies through the ad hoc and episodic display of instances and examples, layers of meaning and eccentricities of confluence, intersection, and congruence. But I maintain that tradition and system cannot share a single throne, and a crown cannot set on two heads or minds at once. Diverse statements of Judaisms will be seen to constitute not traditional but systemic religious documents, with a particular hermeneutics of order, proportion, above all, reasoned context, to tell us how to read each document. We cannot read these writings in accord with two incompatible hermeneutical programs, and, for reasons amply stated, I argue in favor of the philosophical and systemic, rather than the agglutinative and traditional, hermeneutics.

We therefore return, via a circuitous route, to the intersection of the analysis of logic and the characterization of literature as systematic or traditional. For whatever happens to thought, in the mind of the thinker ideas come to birth cogent, whole, complete — and on their own. Extrinsic considerations of context and circumstance play their role, but logic, cogent discourse, rhetoric — these enjoy an existence, an integrity too. If sentences bear meaning on their own, then to insist that sentences bear meaning only in line with their associates, their friends, companions, partners in meaning, contradicts the inner logic of syntax that, on its own, imparts sense to sentences. These are the choices: everything imputed, as against an inner integrity of logic and the syntax of syllogistic thought. But there is no compromise. As between the philosophical heritage of Athens and the hermeneutics of the Judaic tradition known from classical times forward, I maintain that one document of the intellect of Judaism after another in classical times demonstrates the power of the philosophical reading of mind. In the end, the intellect of Judaism in its classic age appealed to the self-evidence of truth compelled by of the well-framed argument, the well-crafted sentence of thought, the orderly cadence of correct, shared, and public logic — that and not the (mere) authority of tradition.

The program and order of inquiry ahead are dictated by what I have argued is the priority of system in the representation of intellect. We have first to identify writings that fall into the classification of systemic statements, and then to analyze the logic(s) of cogent discourse that serve to make those statements in a socially-congruent manner. Among the enormous corpus of writing yielded by the intellect of Judaism in ancient times, I find, representative of the systemic compositions overall, only five documents or collections of documents that realize truly systemic purposes and therefore demand attention as full realizations of the Jewish social intellect: [1] the Pentateuch, [2] the composite collected by the Essenes of Qumran, [3] the Mishnah, and [4] the two Talmuds, of which we shall concentrate on the later. What separates these writings from all others deriving whole or in part from authorships that regarded themselves as, and claimed to address, "Israel" is simple. All of them presented a whole and complete, closed-systemic account of the world-view and the way of life of the Israel they wished to formulate.

That is to say, by referring solely to what they tell us, we may imagine whatever social system and world-order they proposed to invent. That system and order, moreover, takes up each required topic necessary for the exhaustive statement that the authorship at hand wished to make, and omits all topics not necessary for the expression of that same statement. To state matters simply, a system finds cogency in identifying an urgent and encompassing question and proposing a, to the authorship self-evidently valid, answer to that question. We know that a system has completed its work when we can identify the generative problematic the authorship proposes to address and assess whether, in terms of its goals, the authorship at hand has explored the outer limits of that encompassing social problematic. When we read the Pentateuch, the more important Essene writings seen together, the Mishnah, and the Bavli, we can specify the question and the answer: the systemic problematic, the statement that, in brief or at vast length, addresses and resolves that problematic, urgent question, self-evidently valid answer, all together, all at once. And, by the way, these systems dictate also those logics of making connections and drawing conclusions that serve their purpose. So, as it clear, first comes the identification of the systemic writing, then the specification of its interior structure and construction in the specification of ineluctable connections, demanding to be drawn, and self-evidently required conclusions, scarcely requiring apologia. For the intellect of Judaism, for reasons of intellect and not merely tradition, the Pentateuch takes priority, not of temporal order alone, but especially, of excellence of system-building. It defines the royal way. It sets the standard. It forms the criterion for all to follow. And, as a matter of fact, all later system-builders responded to it. So let us start there.

Part Two

Solutions and Their Dilemmas

CHAPTER TEN

INTELLIGIBLE DISCOURSE IN SYSTEMIC CONTEXT: PENTATEUCHAL JUDAISM

The Pentateuch, that is, the Five Books of Moses, forms the first systemic statement in the history of Judaism. For, as we review the canonical Scriptures of ancient Israel, known, for Christianity as the Old Testament, and for Judaism as the Written Torah or Tanakh (made up of T, N and K, standing for the first letters of these words: Torah, the Pentateuch, Nebiim, Prophets, and Ketubim, Writings) or the Written Torah, we find that only one systematic statement reaches full expression, the one presented in the Pentateuch. There alone, among all of the canonical writings of ancient Israel, do we find a full and exhaustive statement of the way of life and world-view of an "Israel." We shall presently review precisely what question finds its answer in the system of Pentateuchal Judaism. Further, once we understand the morphology of the systemic statement undertaken in that composition, its compelling answer to an urgent question present throughout, we shall also account for the logics of cogent discourse present in the Pentateuchal-Judaic system. These are what rendered self-evidently valid, and, of course, intelligible, the making of one set of connections rather than some other, and the drawing of one set of conclusions rather than different ones. For, as is characteristic of any well-crafted system, the whole of the Pentateuchal writings, as they were finally arranged and put together, is so aimed at making a single cogent statement. Only when we can identify that statement shall we find our way toward the inner structures that impart to that statement proportion, composition, logical relationship, and — it follows — cogency. For, as I have argued, the order of the formation of the intellect is from the whole to the parts. That is to say, the systemic statement defines the logic needed to make that statement. The manner of making connections and drawing conclusions does not percolate upward into the framing of the systemic statement.

Let us first consider my claim that, among all of the canonical writings of ancient Israel now before us, only the Pentateuch constitutes, and presents, a system. That is to say, alone in the Pentateuch do we find an encompassing and cogent statement composed of an account of a way of life, a world-view, and an "Israel" that in its everyday life realizes the one and accounts for its society and, therefore, its history through the other. It is the simple fact that all other scriptural writings stand in relationship to that system au fond. They either are arranged in succession to, therefore in relationship with, that system, for example, the historical books, Joshua, Judges, Samuel, and Kings. Or they make no pretense at exhibiting a systemic character at all. In all other scriptural books we look in vain, for example, for a picture of how people are to live, of who they are as a social entity, of the way the world is composed and to be explained. The compilers of Jeremiah, the authors of Psalms, the collectors of Proverbs — these estimable circles in no way provide the prescription for an entire social world.

True, there is Ezekiel 40-48, the counterpart to the Pentateuchal description in Leviticus of the cult. What we find, in a fragmentary way, underlines the uniqueness as a systemic statement, within the Hebrew Scriptures, of the Pentateuch. While the Priestly Code and related writings go on to describe the world arrayed around the cult, Ezekiel 40-48 ignores by treating only by indirection and implicit judgment the enveloping web of social relationships defined in detail by the priestly authorship. Ezekiel attends by explicit statement only to the structure of society within, and in relationship to the cult itself; the detail is lacking. The statement of hierarchization expressed through the cult completed, everything else is left to inference. But a systemic statement invariably speaks blatantly, repetitiously, boringly, and explicitly, saying its message over and over again in innumerable ways, but never by mere inference. What Ezekiel 40-48 omits but the Priestly Code encompasses marks the frontier between a truncated, and merely suggestive, outline of what someone might wish to conceive and set forth and a systemic statement. That contrast explains why the Pentateuch as now put together, in the "Five Books of Moses," in fact, the Pentateuchal mosaic, forms the only candidate for classification as a system, so far as I can discern, in the entire corpus of canonical prophecy.

True, prophetic compilations, for instance, Isaiah, Jeremiah, the Second Isaiah, and Ezekiel, take for granted not only a society but also a social system. They appeal to both ethos and ethics, shared values and a common way of life. But they make no systemic statement. A sustained critique of a system is not a systemic statement but, like a vine on a trellis, simply lies heavy upon a system. Such a critique hardly permits us to impute to prophecy a conception of a social order that accounts for how things are, addressing the relationships and institutions of society, the conceptions that account for the origins and authority of those institutions and givenness of those relationships. Either proposing to criticize in the name of those shared values an incongruent reality, or offering in judgment upon the existing society an explicitly fictive account of a better system that will some day be realized within Israel through God's intervention, prophets never undertake the work of system-builders. They presuppose, they allude to, they depend upon, but they never compose and set forth a well-proportioned and complete composition of their "Israel," its worldview and way of life, in the way in which the Pentateuchal compilers did after 586 and before 450 B.C. As to the Writings, read as statements meant to realize, in a social system, a well-composed statement and intent, these prove at best episodic. The books of Psalms, Proverbs, Job, Song of Songs, Lamentations, and the like address diverse circumstances. Ad hoc and free-standing, none can be set forth as systemic in contents or in character.

But, read in the context of the age in which they were put together as a whole, that is, in the sixth century B.C. the Five Books of Moses, Genesis, Exodus, Leviticus, Numbers, and Deuteronomy, can. The history of the Pentateuch as a systematic statement begins with the ultimate formation into a cogent composite of diverse writings. Where those materials came from, for whom they spoke to begin with, what they meant prior to their restatement in the context and system they now comprise, define questions the answers to which have no bearing whatsoever upon the systemic analysis of those same writings. For the system begins whole, and what system-builders do with received materials is whatever they wish to do with them. They do not recognize themselves as bound by prior and original authors' intent, and neither are we so bound in interpreting the outcome of the work of composition and (re)statement. Read, therefore, as a continuous and also complete statement, the Pentateuchal mosaic forms a system with an origin (Eden, Sinai) but without a secular history (this king, that king), addressed to a present that has only a future, but no pertinent past. But even when read in that way, does the Pentateuchal mosaic conform to the definition of a system just now given? And how shall we know? In the two requisite dimensions of such a definition, world-view and way of life, it does, and in the other indicative trait of a system, social focus and intent, it does as well.

For the Pentateuchal mosaic, composite though it is, has been so formed as to frame a question and answer that question, forming remarkably disparate materials into a statement of coherence and order. The question that is answered encompasses a variety of issues, but it always is one question: who is Israel in relationship to the land? In the aftermath of 586, the "exile," followed by ca. 530, the "return to Zion," that question certainly demanded attention among those few whose families had both gone into exile and returned to

Zion, and the Pentateuchal mosaic was compiled by the priests among them in particular as an account of the Temple, cult, and priesthood in the center and heart of the way of life, world-view, and social entity of the particular "Israel" the priests proposed to make up. That explains why the question from beginning in Genesis to conclusion at the eve of entry into the land in Deuteronomy is, what are the conditions for the formation of the union of Israel with the enchanted land it is to occupy? It also accounts for the ineluctable and persuasive character of the answer, once again encompassing a variety of details: the Pentateuchal "Israel," defined by genealogy, like the priesthood, formed the family become holy people, and that genealogical "Israel" possesses the land by reason of the covenant of its fathers-founders, Abraham, Isaac, and Jacob. That covenant is given detail and substance with the forming of the people at Sinai. Israel the people possesses the land not as a given but as a gift, subject to stipulations. The fundamental systemic statement repetitiously and in one detail after another answers the question of why Israel has lost the land of Israel and what it must do to hold on to it once again. Accordingly, in a single statement we may set forth the systemic message: God made the land and gave it to Israel on condition that Israel do what God demands. That is the answer. It also leads us to define the ineluctable question, that demands this answer, the question that presses and urgently insists upon an answer. In the circumstance, after the destruction of the Temple of Jerusalem in 586 B.C., of the formation of the Pentateuchal composition and system, the question is equally accessible. It is, why has Israel lost the land, and what does Israel have to do now to hold on to it again?

    The Pentateuchal system, taking shape in the aftermath of the exile to Babylonia in 586 and reaching closure with the return to Zion some decades later finds urgent the question framed by that rather small number of Israelite families who remembered the exile, survived in Babylonia, and then, toward the end of the sixth and fifth centuries B.C., returned to Zion, knew things that enlandised Israel before 586 could never have imagined. The system of Judaism that would predominate therefore began by making a selection of facts to be deemed consequential, hence historical, and by ignoring, in the making of that selection, the experiences of others who had a quite different perception of what had happened. And, as a matter of fact, that selection of systemically important facts dictated the making of connections, that is, the joining of this fact to that fact, rather than to some other. For once the system-builders know the facts they wish to address, they also will discern connections between those facts and no others. The logic of connection depends upon the logic of drawing conclusions from connection. And conclusions derive from a prior recognition of questions we wish to answer. For one example, I may posit, by way of a mental experiment, a simple case: the connection between the destruction of the Temple, the exile to Babylonia, and the return to Zion, will not have struck a family that remained in Babylonia as self-evident; for that family did not return to Zion. To such thought as such a family devoted to their social circumstances, the return to Zion will have proved not an inevitable and ineluctable event, this, then that, this, joined to that. In such system as it formed, that fact will have proved inert, hence not part of the joints of the construction as a whole.

That is why I claim that the connections deemed ineluctable began with the system, not with the details. The facts found noteworthy to begin with found consequence in the system that identified those facts and not other facts. And the one fact that the ones who came back, and, by definition, many of those who were taken away, were priests made all the difference, as the books of Ezra and Nehemiah indicate. For to the priests the fate of the Temple defined what mattered in 586. The destruction of the Temple defined that web of social relationships and connections that joined one thing to something else and set the whole into hierarchical order. It had to follow, then, that what made the difference, what was at stake, "three generations later" was not alone the restoration of Israel to the land, but the rebuilding of the Temple. The former not connected to the latter made no sense. And that connection, people to land through temple, formed the generative problematic of the system as a whole, accounting, as a matter of fact, for the bulk of the materials included in the

Pentateuch and for the way in which those materials are laid out. To the Pentateuchal system the cult was the key, the Temple (in mythic language then) the nexus between heaven and earth. The Five Books of Moses composed as its systemic statement an account of the unsettling encounter with annihilation avoided, extinction postponed, life renewed — Temple restored as portrayed in P's Leviticus and Numbers. To Israel the Torah imparted the picture of society subject to judgment. And it was the priests' judgment in particular that prevailed.

What conclusion was to be drawn from that generative pattern of connection that the system put forth? It was that the system's "Israel's" life was, as I said, itself not a given but a gift. The system's "Israel" stood for a group that at any time might lose its land, so that the relation to the land, the foundation of social existence was turned into the basis for and indicator of the group's moral existence as well. The principal givens of the Pentateuchal Torah's systemic paradigm, namely, its "Israel's" heightened sense of its own social reality, its status as an elected people standing in a contractual or covenantal relationship with God, propositions of both the Torah and the historical and prophetic writings of the century beyond 586, in fact speak out of inner structure of the system. True, after millennia of repetition, we take for granted the givenness of the systemic propositions. But once they were fresh assertions, contradicting other views (which we can scarcely reconstruct) and answering burning questions. Accordingly, these systemic givens as a matter of fact express the system's logic, not a logic intrinsic in events, even in events selected and reworked. The givens frame the system's premises, not the data of Israel's common life in either Babylonia, to which they were simply irrelevant, or the Land of Israel, among those who never went into "exile," and who found themselves subject to the judgment of those who had gone and come back. For the system not only selected the events it would deem consequential. It also selected those events that would not form connections to one another and so would not yield conclusions, and that would, therefore, prove, in an exact sense of the word, inconsequential: not-connected and therefore not significant.

Let us dwell on this matter of a systemic judgment upon the given society, for it shows with great clarity the standing and viewpoint of the system-builders. Specifically, what we now understand is that the system-builders did not describe the given social world but proposed to create afresh, out of their own minds first of all, a society that should come to realization. From the perspective of a vast Israelite population, namely, Jews who had remained in the land, Jews who had never left Babylonia, Jews living in other parts of the world, such as Egypt, the system spoke of events that simply had never happened or had not happened in the way that the Pentateuchal mosaic claims. For the systemic conclusions invoked no self-evidently valid connections, when people had no data out of their own, or their family's, experience, on the basis of which to make such connections. Consider the Jews who remained in the land after 586, or those who remained in Babylonia after Cyrus's decree permitting the return to Zion. For both groups, for different reasons, there was no alienation, also, consequently, no reconciliation, and the normative corresponded to the merely normal: life like any other nation, wherever it happened to locate itself. And that ignores Jews in Egypt, Mesopotamia, and other parts of the world of the time, who were not in the Land when it was captured and who also were not taken captive to Babylonia.

True enough, treating exile and return as the generative problematic and therefore as normative imparted to the exile the critical and definitive position. It marked Israel as special, elect, subject to the rules of the covenant and its stipulations. But, as we now realize, for much of Israel, some system other than the system of the normative alienation constructed by the Judaism of the Torah will have to have enjoyed that self-evidence that, for the (priestly) exiles returned, the system of the Torah possessed. For to them who stayed put, the urgent question of exile and return, the self-evidently valid response of election and covenant, bore slight relevance, asked no questions worth asking, provided no answers worth believing. When we want an example of a religious system creating a society, we can find few better instances than the power of the conception of Israel expressed by the Pentateuch and associated writings, of the period after 586 B.C., to tell people not only the meaning of what had happened but what had happened: to create for Israelite society a picture of what it must be and therefore had been.

That sense of heightened reality, that intense focus on the identification of the nation as extraordinary, represented only one possible picture of the meaning of events from 586 B.C. onward. But we do not have access to any other but the system of the Torah. And the system of the Torah after 586 did not merely describe things that had actually happened, systemically inert facts, so to speak, but made a choice among such inert or "normal" events, rendering some of them normative and mythic, turning an experience into a paradigm of experience. The system defined the events that mattered and, we now see clearly, therefore dictated the kinds of connections it would discern, and, it goes without saying, also, therefore, the conclusions it would draw. The systemic paradigm began as a paradigm, not as a set of actual events that people saw as connected and that they then transformed into a normative pattern. And the conclusions generated by the paradigm, it must follow, derived not from reflection on things that happened but from the logic of the paradigm. Accordingly, the system comes prior to the logic that forms its interior structure and defines its inner proportions and composition.

What follows is simple. First came the system, its world-view and way of life formed whole we know not where or by whom. Then came the selection, by the system, of consequential events and their patterning into systemic propositions. That is the point at which systemic logic enters. And finally, at a third stage (of indeterminate length of time) came the formation and composition of the canon that would express the logic of the system and state those "events" that the system would select or invent for its own expression. And that is the stage at which a self-conscious positioning of a system vis-à-vis inherited systems takes place. We have now dealt with the first two matters — the system and its consequent logic of making connections and drawing conclusions. Let us now turn to the issue of how the framers presented their work, specifically, whether or not the system-builders who made the Pentateuchal Judaism presented their system as (merely) traditional or as a free-standing system. The answer to the question is not that they inherited and made use of available materials, "traditions." That is beside the point. What we want to know concerns the system, and not the raw materials of which it was composed, and that is a quite different matter. Specifically, does the Pentateuchal authorship represent its work as a statement of a tradition, out of the long-ago past, or does it present its statement as an essentially autonomous statement, whole and complete on its own? That is the question at hand.

The fulcrum on which the system rests is its social entity, its "Israel," and that "Israel" in the Pentateuchal system refers not to a natural past, generations of descent family by family, but an act of selection of one family and its descendants, a very different thing. Since, chief among the propositions of the system as the Torah of Moses defined it is the notion of the election of Israel effected in the covenant, we may say that, systemically speaking, Israel — the Israel of the Torah and historical-prophetic books of the sixth and fifth centuries — selected itself. The system created the paradigm of the society that had gone into exile and come back home, and, by the way, the system also cut its own orders, that contract or covenant that certified not election but self-selection. A particular experience, transformed by a religious system into a paradigm of the life of the social group, has become normative and therefore generative. But — to repeat the central point — that particular experience itself happened, to begin with, in the minds and imaginations of the authorship of the Pentateuch as we have it, not in the concrete life or in the politics and society of Israel in its land and in exile. The same is so for a long list of systemic givens, none of them, as a matter of fact, matters of self-evidence except to those to whom they were self-evident.

That is why a large portion of the Pentateuch devotes time and attention to the matter of the cult, that is to say, the centrality of sacrifice, the founding of the priesthood and its rules, and the importance of the Temple in Jerusalem. That is why many of the stories of Genesis are aimed at explaining the origin, in the lives and deeds of the patriarchs, of the locations of various cultic centers prior to the centralization of the cult in Jerusalem, the beginnings of the priesthood, the care and feeding of priests, the beginnings and rules of the sacrificial system, the contention between priestly castes, e.g., Levites and priests, and diverse other matters. Much of Exodus is devoted to the description of the tabernacle in the wilderness as prototype of the Temple. Leviticus and much of Numbers are devoted to the same topic. Deuteronomy, the most compendious and encompassing of the composites, pays ample attention to the matter. But what is important is not the centrality of the cult to the systemic statement as a whole. Rather the system links the whole of the social order to the cult, and that is what imparts to the system its distinctive structure and conveys its urgent messages. The picture of the system's Israel, its "kingdom of priests" ruled by priests, its "holy people" living out the holiness imparted by obedience to the covenant, as a matter of fact laid claim to the authority of God's revelation to Moses at Sinai. But, of course, "Sinai" stood for Babylonia. There the priests drew together the elements of the received picture and reshaped them into the fairly coherent set of rules and narratives for the social order, the account of the social entity, "Israel," its way of life, its world-view, that we now know as the Pentateuch. All of this is represented as given, revealed by God to Moses at Sinai. And nothing is presented as tradition formed out of a long chain of incremental and sedimentary formation. It was all together, all at once, one time, with no past other than the past made up for the system, not process, not justified by ancient custom. The ideology of the statement appeals to the opposite of tradition: revelation, of which Pentateuchal Scripture is the exhaustive record, and that alone. I point, therefore, to the system's explanation of its own origins in a single act of revelation as the stunningly final judgment of its own character: not a (mere) tradition, preserved by mortals, but a system, a revelation, set forth by God to Moses once for all time. True, systems can and have set forth other indicators of their judgment of themselves, and they need not appeal to a one-time revelation to impute to themselves systemic and not traditional standing. But for the Pentateuchal Judaism, the appeal to Sinai suffices to state the Judaism's definitive character as a system, not as a tradition in any sense the authorship at hand can have understood.

This brings us to the center of matters, the system itself. If I am correct that the Pentateuchal Judaism makes a statement, I should be able to repeat it in a simple and cogent way. We have in hand a most convenient statement of the systemic message as a whole. The priests' vision, attaching to the Pentateuchal system as a whole, is characterized as follows:

> In the priests' narrative the chosen people are last seen as pilgrims moving through alien land toward a goal to be fulfilled in another time and place, and this is the vision, drawn from the ancient story of their past, that the priests now hold out to the scattered sons and daughters of old Israel. They too are exiles encamped for a time in an alien land, and they too must focus their hopes on the promise ahead. Like the Israelites in the Sinai wilderness, they must avoid setting roots in the land through which they pass, for Diaspora is not to become their permanent condition, and regulations must be adopted to facilitate this. They must resist assimilation into the world into which they are now dispersed, because hope and heart and fundamental identity lay in the future. Thus, the priestly document not only affirms Yahweh's continuing authority and action in the lives of his people but offers them a pattern for life that will ensure them a distinct identity.[1]

The net effect of the Pentateuchal vision of Israel, that is, its world-view seen in the aggregate, lays stress on the separateness and the holiness of Israel, all the while pointing to dangers of pollution by the other, the outsider. The way of life, with its stress on distinguishing traits of an Israel distinct from, and threatened by, the outsider corresponds. The fate of the nation, moreover, depends upon the loyalty of the people, in their everyday life, to the requirements of the covenant with God, so history forms the barometer of the health of the

---

[1] W. Lee Humphreys, Crisis and Story. Introduction to the Old Testament (Palo Alto: Mayfield Publishing Co., 1979), p. 217. I choose Humphreys's statement not only because of its authority, but also because it speaks for a considerable scholarly consensus, serving, after all, as a textbook account of what, in general, people now think.

nation. In these ways the several segments of the earlier traditions of Israel were so drawn together as to make the point peculiarly pertinent to Israel in exile. It follows that the original Judaic system, the one set forth by the Pentateuch, answered the urgent issue of exile with the self-evident response of return. The question was not to be avoided, the answer not to be doubted. The center of the system, then, lay in the covenant, the contract that told Israel the rules that would govern: Keep these rules and you will not again suffer as you have suffered. Violate them and you will. At the heart of the covenant was the call for Israel to form a kingdom of priests and a holy people.

That brings us back, via a circuitous route, to the matter of the logic of cogent discourse, that matter of principles of making connections and drawing conclusions that I have stressed as the inner building blocks of the intellect of Judaism. Within my theory of systemic analysis of logic, we should be able to find, in any passage or set of passages, evidence of a single persistent mode of making connections and drawing conclusions. Where to begin? The starting point is dictated by the logics of intelligible discourse, that is, modes of making connection. The Pentateuchal system clearly rejects the philosophical, and chooses the teleological approach to finding out how one thing links up with some other and to drawing conclusions from that connection. We know that the choice of types of facts for connection time and again falls upon what are deemed to be events, and, in consequence, the principal mode of sustained discourse is the telling of stories. The world-view of the system emerges in particular through these stories. When the system-builders wish to account for the identification of the social entity, "Israel," they tell the story of the founders, the patriarchs and matriarchs, and what happened to them. "Israel" then comes into being through the story of how the family became the people. The laws of the system, its way of life, are set forth within a narrative setting, e.g., revelation at Sinai, in Exodus, the circumstance and the speaker and the authority, in Leviticus and Numbers. Not only so, but even where the laws are laid out essentially independent of narrative, as in Deuteronomy, the laws as a whole are laid out in a tight relationship to a story, so that the fictive setting provides what the system deems absolutely essential. In these and other instances we discern the system's general conception, that connection derives from sequence, first this, then that, hence that is because of this. Then the drawing of conclusions derives from connections discerned between this and that: one event, then another event, and the cause that links the latter to the former and explains the order of things.

From generalization we move to an instance of concrete speech. There we shall see that teleological logic, dictating the connections we make and the conclusions we draw, appeals not only to history, though we entered that logic through the door of history. Teleology appeals to goal or purpose, of which history forms a mere example. What links together the sentences that follow is the goal stated at the outset. In achieving this goal, these are the things that one must do. Then a set of discrete sentences, not topically or logically related to one another at all, follows. And each sentence finds its place in context for the same reason. It is another way to achieve that purpose set forth at the head. Lev. 19:1-18 (given in the Revised Standard Version) provides our instance of teleological connection among otherwise unrelated facts/sentences:

> And the Lord said to Moses, "Say to all the congregation of the people of Israel, You shall be holy, for I the Lord your God am holy.
> "Every one of you shall revere his mother and his father and you shall keep my Sabbaths, I am the Lord your God.
> "Do not turn to idols or make for yourselves molten gods; I am the Lord your God.
> "When you offer a sacrifice of peace offerings to the Lord, you shall offer it so that you may be accepted. It shall be eaten the same day you offer it or on the morrow, and anything left over until the third day shall be burned with fire. If it is eaten at all on the third day, it is an abomination, it will not be accepted, and everyone who eats it shall bear his iniquity, because he has profaned a holy thing of the Lord; and that person shall be cut off from his people.
> "When you reap the harvest of your land, you shall not reap

> your field to its very border, neither shall you gather the gleanings after your harvest. And you shall not strip your vineyard bare, neither shall you gather the fallen grapes of your vineyard; you shall leave them for the poor and for the sojourner. I am the Lord your God.
> "You shall not steal, nor deal falsely, nor lie to one another. And you shall not swear by my name falsely and so profane the name of your God; I am the Lord. You shall not oppress your neighbor or rob him. The wages of a hired servant shall not remain with you all night until the morning. You shall not curse the deaf or put a stumbling block before the blind, but you shall fear your God; I am the Lord.
> "You shall do no injustice in judgment; you shall not be partial to the poor or defer to the great, but in righteousness shall you judge your neighbor. You shall not go up and down as a slanderer among your people, and you shall not stand forth against the life of your neighbor; I am the Lord.
> "You shall not hate your brother in your heart, but you shall reason with your neighbor, lest you bear sin because of him. You shall not take vengeance or bear any grudge against the sons of your own people, but you shall love your neighbor as yourself; I am the Lord."

Except for the opening and closing lines of the pericope, the linkage of sentence to sentence (treating the paragraphs as sentences) is hardly self-evident. These are all things that, unrelated to one another, relate to the goal of sanctification. This mixture of rules we should regard as cultic, as to sacrifice, moral, as to support of the poor, ethical, as to right-dealing, and above all religious, as to "being holy for I the Lord your God am holy" — the rules all together portray a complete and whole society: its world-view, holiness in the likeness of God, its way of life, an everyday life of sanctification through the making of distinctions, its Israel: Israel. The definition of who is Israel lay at the foundation of the system, which was shaped to answer that urgent question of social explanation. That is what holds the whole together, and, we see, the principle of cogent discourse appeals to teleology expressed as a kind of narrative.

But making connection in the teleological manner is not only dictated by the goals of an abstract order we have just reviewed. Connections link one event to another, one act to another, and, most important, an act to an event. Accordingly, the teleological logic of connection, and, necessarily, of conclusion as well, will appeal to what the framers conceive to be the ineluctable union between the actions of persons and the events that affect the society they form. "If you do this, that will happen," forms a statement linking an action to a social and historical result, and that forms, in another dimension, a teleological connection as well. Thus: "If you walk in my statutes and observe my commandments and do them, then I will give you your rains in their season" (Lev. 26:3), "but if you will not hearken to me and will not do all these commandments, ...I will do this to you: I will appoint over you sudden terror...and you shall sow your seed in vain for your enemies shall eat it...Then the land shall enjoy its Sabbaths as long as it lies desolate while you are in your enemies' land...." (Lev. 26:34). That teleology of connection and conclusion tells us what facts join what other facts, and what conclusions we are to draw in consequence. It is a uniform logic, and the structure of the Pentateuchal intellect seems to me remarkably cogent.

The Pentateuchal system made its statement not only through the conclusions it set forth, but also through the processes of thought that after the fact generated these conclusions. It defined as its generative question the loss of the land and its restoration to and retention by Israel. It answered the question of how to prevent the events of the recent past from happening ever again. It gave as its answer the formation of a separate and holy society, an Israel. Events, the connections between and among them, the conclusions to be drawn from those connections, defined the focus of interest, because the system treated as urgent a question defined by what had happened to the "Israel" that the system chose to address. The Judaic system of the Pentateuch confronted the overwhelming question of the meaning of what had happened and supplied the (to the priests') self-evidently valid answer: Israel must obey the rules of holiness, and, if it does, then by keeping its half of the agreement or covenant, it could make certain God would find valid the other half: "And I will give peace in the land, and you shall lie down and none shall make you afraid" (Lev. 26:6).

That accounts, also, for the logic of intelligible discourse that served that system so well.

The satisfying sense of composition, proportion, and order conveyed by the Pentateuchal system finds no counterpart afterward, as we shall now see. No other Judaic system would remotely succeed as did the Pentateuchal system in its systemic cogency, in its completeness and order, in its sense of the correspondence of ethos to ethics, in its power to generate a logic fitting to the systemic statement. The intellect of Judaism began at its pinnacle of success. No wonder that, to the rightly pleased authorship of the Pentateuchal Judaism, viewing the results of their handiwork, a sufficient pseudepigraphic attribution for aesthetic, not only political, reasons, could be only to God on high, through Moses as mere tradent. The modesty of situating themselves merely as last and least in a line of tradition was systemically beyond imagining. Such forthright pride in their achievement in system-building from a secular angle of vision is entirely justified. For, from the system-builders' perspective on what they had made, as a matter of simple fact only God could have wrought it. No Judaic system-builders ever disagreed with them, though all would tacitly reject their system as it came forth by rereading, each authorship in its terms, what had come forth as a closed and completed system, that is to say, "from Sinai."

Chapter Eleven

System and Cogency at Qumran

Whether or not the Judaism set forth by the library at Qumran reveals a system forms the question before us. The answer is not self-evident. True, we can construct a picture of their ethos. We can spell out in a reasonably coherent way an account of their ethics. We can surely state what we conceive their "Israel" to have been and not to have been. But in the library at Qumran, we have no way of saying whether or not, in seeing the whole as a system, we are right. That is to say, what we have in hand are merely parts, which *can* have served a systemic statement. But what people might have made of these things, and what they did make of them, are different matters, and we can judge the answer we make up only to the first of those two questions. The task of systemic study is the analysis, not the invention, of systems. So in the end, our judgment of the library of Qumran rests upon the form in which these materials reach us. If not sewn together, but in discrete documents, if not formed into a sustained and coherent statement, but only made up, one by one, each for its occasion, then, as we shall see, we have something less than a cogent system, if clearly more than a mere potpourri of writings. A Judaism comparable to the Judaism of the Pentateuch, moreover, will appeal to a logic of cogent discourse that clearly relates to the larger systemic program, such as we find not only in the Pentateuch's teleological logic but also in the Mishnah's taxonomic logic of comparison and contrast. Absent such a clear correlation of logic and system, we really cannot claim to describe the intellect of a Judaism. Knowing our criterion, let us see whether the Qumran library writings meet it.

If the Pentateuchal Judaism sets the standard for the definition of a system, then the writings discovered as the Judaic system set forth by the library at Qumran on the surface hardly measure up. For while the Judaic system set forth by the library at Qumran adumbrates a system and exhibits a certain cogency of logical discourse, the documents do not hold together in the remarkably coherent way in which the diverse writings assembled in the Pentateuchal mosaic do. Not only so, but, as a matter of fact, we do not know that the library's documents were meant to constitute a system, and, consequently, we cannot impute to them a systemically indicative logic at all. There is a further obstacle to accepting the claim that the writings found at Qumran (and elsewhere) form a systemic statement. The reason is this: when we read some of the principal writings and ask whether they conform to the indicative traits of a system, we hardly find self-evident the presence of those systemic indicators that so impress even a casual reader of the Pentateuch as a system.

All we know for sure about the writings of the library discovered (mainly) at Qumran is that they were found acceptable to the community whose librarians collected those writings. But we do not know why, or for what purpose, the documents proved acceptable. Whether or not the writings on that account comprise a system in the way that the Pentateuch does, we cannot show; presently I shall propose to demonstrate the very opposite. For the work of collecting writings is different from the labor of compiling, for the purposes of an identifiable group, as a single, sustained statement, a composite of (originally) diverse writings coming from we know not where. That is precisely what the authorship of the Pentateuch did but what was not attempted for the collection of writings found at Qumran. Recognizing that distinction between a (mere) library and a composite statement of a system deriving from a distinct group forms a critical component of the argument of this book about the formation of the intellect of Judaism. For the distinction instructs us on where we may identify the work of a social intellect, available for description, analysis and interpretation, and where we may not find it at all. The writings assembled as the Pentateuch form a continuous account, beginning to end. Those in the Qumran library are not utterly autonomous of one another and are surely connected by more points of intersection than the mere act of librarians in placing them on the same shelf (so to speak). But they assuredly exhibit no continuities that require us to read them from some putative beginning to some alleged end.

Let me state the distinction negatively, then positively. A book is not a system, and a collection of books is not the statement of a system. Let me offer a working definition of the difference between a (mere) collection of books and a systemic statement in literary form. A work that purports to speak in an anonymous voice, not only to, but also for, an entire social entity (or for a prophet in the name of God to that entity), presents a system, in accord with a simple criterion that can be tested. The presentation of a system succeeds in such measure as, in that continuous, uniform voice, for that entity, the writing fully exposes the ethics, ethos, and identification of the social entity. By that criterion a mosaic of compiled materials such as the Pentateuch assuredly presents a systemic statement A collection of autonomous writings, compiled adventitiously and merely preserved by decision of some authority or other, does not. For a library represents a conglomerate of (presumably) acceptable writings, a mosaic of writings presented as a single, continuous statement constitutes a deliberately composed document, a composite meant to hold together and therefore one that has been deliberately put together. The difference between a library and a system in the form of a literary mosaic such as the Pentateuch is the difference between a set of approved writings and (in deliberately anachronistic terms) a publicly acknowledged theology, a pattern of truth, and, in the context of the intellect of Judaism beginning with the Pentateuch, a social system comprising ethos and ethics addressed to a distinct social entity. And the two really do not compare with one another.

For the Qumran librarians (again to speak in anachronism) have merely placed the stamp of their approval upon items they have chosen to collect and preserve, and what they approved so far as we know as fact is solely the preservation of those items. We cannot claim to know their purpose, let alone the value they imputed to the writings at hand. By contrast, the authorship of a mosaic such as the Pentateuch has undertaken an utterly different exercise. That authorship pretends to speak in one voice, to set forth a seamless discourse, to say some one thing: a pattern of truth, an orthodoxy as against a heterodoxy, so to speak, again, somewhat anachronistically. In concrete terms, we have in the model of the Pentateuch only a few systemic counterparts. But, for the Qumran library, we have many equivalent collections. For only a few authorships within Jewry expressed their ideas in a shared and public composite, one voice for many, while the identification and the preservation of authoritative writings went forward wherever individuals or groups had the means to do so. True, not just anyone could make a library, but fewer still could accomplish the feat of authorship represented by the Pentateuch.

This point becomes clear when we contrast with the canonical Hebrew Scriptures/Old Testament, in all its diversity of voice, intent, genre, and message, the Pentateuch, the authorship of which pretended to tell a single uninterrupted story in a single voice. The chosen voice of the Pentateuch is that of Moses. The authorities and also the Judaic and the Christian canonical theologians who identified certain ancient writings as authoritative for the synagogue and the Church and so made the canon as we have it by contrast in no way claimed to say some one thing in a single voice. Quite to the contrary, they laid down a different judgment by certifying as divinely revealed or inspired various writings that they preserved in all their individuality and acknowledged diversity. The upshot is simple. The work of identifying a canon of approved writings made no pretense at joining all things into one thing.

The authorship of the Pentateuch, by contrast, took many sources and turned them, with considerable ingenuity, into one statement. In that way that authorship did more than impart to the diverse writings authoritative status as divinely revealed. The authorship gained for its writing the standing of a single, continuous, cogent, whole statement, and that in the nature of things represents a different sort of standing all together. It was the standing of the one message (in later, mythic, terms, "the one whole Torah") revealed to Moses by God and handed on by Moses as tradition. By joining the various available sources into a single statement, the authorship of the Pentateuch presented as unitary tradition from Sinai whatever they had chosen to select as authoritative. In so doing, that authorship accordingly did more than compile writings, it created a system. This was done by pasting together everything into a single cogent statement, all in one place, of a world-view and a way of life addressed to a defined social entity and intended to answer with compelling, self-evident truth an urgent question.

Now the work of identifying diverse writings only as uniformly canonical is one thing. Forming and presenting them in a single cogent statement is quite another. And, as between the two different ways of disposing of inherited writings, the authorities behind the selection of materials discovered at Qumran accomplished the former. But even here, the issue is not fully settled. For, as I said at the outset, we cannot say for certain that the authorities of the Qumran community deemed valid and therefore also in harmony with all others every statement of every writing that turned up in their collection. We do not know their motives in regard to selecting and preserving each of the documents. We may well imagine that, just as we identify points of difference between one writing and another, or at least, diverse emphases and interests, not all of them self-evidently harmonious, so did they. Accordingly, we cannot read all the writings associates with the Library of Qumran as though we had in hand nothing more than the counterpart to the Pentateuchal statement of the Priestly system of ca. 450 B.C.

Nonetheless, the library of Qumran demands attention in the context of our analysis of the formation of the intellect of Judaism. The reason is that among the books collected there, we do find components of what, were they written down all together and all at once, we should have deemed on the face of it a highly cogent systemic statement.

Accordingly, I shall compile such a reasonably cogent and harmonious statement by joining together some of the principal assertions of the library's contents. For, as a matter of fact, those represented by the library found at the commune at Qumran preserved writings that do present us with something very like the statement of a system, comprising a view of ethos, ethics, social entity, a compelling answer to an urgent question — all that, and not merely a theology or a philosophy. The reason to ask, to begin with, whether or not we have not a library but a system, is that we have sufficient evidence to describe this sect in its broader social context, not merely as statements of some author's belief. Let us now turn to the library of Qumran and briefly examine its plan and program.

A description of the main programmatic lines of those represented by the Qumran Library yields a few simple observations. The main component of the world-view of the Qumran Judaism was the conviction that the community formed the final remnant of Israel, and that God would shortly annihilate the wicked. These "converts" to the true faith would be saved, because their founder, the teacher of righteousness, established a new contract or covenant between the community and God. So this "Israel" would endure. The task of the community was to remain faithful to the contract or covenant, endure the exile in the wilderness, and prepare for the restoration of the Temple in its correct form. So the community before us recapitulated the history of Israel, seeing itself as the surviving remnant of some disaster that had destroyed the faith, preparing for that restoration that they anticipated would soon come — just as it had before. The collectors represented a Jewish sect that laid emphasis on purity-rules in eating their meals and in conducting their sexual life. They flourished in the last two centuries B.C. down to A.D. 68. The Library of Qumran turned back to the Priestly Code and its generative symbols and myths. Their library's literary statements make constant reference to issues of the Priestly Code.

One encompassing example of that fact is stress upon cultic cleanness and uncleanness, preservation of food and of meals in conditions required, in the Priestly Code of Leviticus and Numbers, only for the Temple and the priests. The members of the sect wanted to obey the rules of holiness, as they applied to the Temple, even while rejecting the Jerusalem temple and maintaining that it in no way realized the vision of the Priestly Code. Accordingly, the Library of Qumran observed a set of rules of cultic cleanness when eating their meals. The group defined itself around the eating of cultic meals in the state of cleanness prescribed by Leviticus for Temple priest in the eating of their share of the Temple sacrifices. In all, therefore, we find in the Qumran system a replication of the structure of the Judaic system of the priesthood, with one important qualification. While the Judaic system represented by the Pentateuch laid great stress on the holy way of life, the Qumran system as represented by its library, added a powerful element of eschatological expectation and so combined with the holy way of life a doctrine of salvation at the end of time. The principal components of the scriptural composite — Torah-laws, prophetic historical-interpretation, sagacious rules on the conduct of everyday life, found counterparts in the library of the Qumran community. That Judaism reworked the several strands into a distinctive and characteristic statement of its own.

Among the more important documents kept in the Qumran library are, first the Community Rule (also called the Manual of Discipline), a handbook of instruction for the head of the community, which outlines the aims of the group and provides a picture of the rite of entering the covenant of the community. Those who join the sect live a holy life, and all others are allies of Satan. The postulates are marked by the spirit of truth or falsehood, the spirit of light or darkness, and the master has to know the difference. The code then provides rules for the life of the community, and these rules are meant to apply until the Messiah comes. It ends with a hymn of thanksgiving.

The master of the Dead Sea Library, Geza Vermes[2] compares the Community Rule to the counterpart rules of Christian monasticism, which define the life of the community. At the end of time, the sect's affairs will be taken over by two Messiahs, one of Israel, one of Aaron (the priesthood). The messianic rule describes the life of the individual from childhood education to marriage to participation in the everyday life of the group and in its militia.

The Community Scroll spends much time describing the institutions of the community beginning with the Council of the Community or assembly of the Congregation. Vermes states, "From a passage ordering all the members to sit in their correct places..., it would seem to have been a gathering of the whole community, under the priests and men of importance, with the guardian at the head." A variety of rules governed the social requirements and sanctions of this "Israel," for example, grounds for expulsion. A central topic, as I have already indicated, was the common meals and how they were conducted. The importance of the meal may be gauged from the fact that a recurrent sanction involved ostracism, meaning, exclusion from the pure meal. A further set of elaborate rules governed entry into the community, a novitiate for a year, followed by a further year of trial. Ample attention, moreover, is paid to the supreme authority of the "Israel," its administration, power, responsibilities, and the like. The Guardian of the community forms a central topic. A sizable body of rules of public conduct is included, indeed the Damascus Covenant presents a set of small but highly systematic pictures of socially permitted behavior of various sorts. Those responsible for the Library of Qumran responded to their own social circumstance, isolated and alone as it was, and formed a community unto itself, hence seeing their "Israel," the social entity of their system, as what there was left of Scripture's "Israel," that is, the remnant of Israel.

---

[2] Geza Vermes, *The Dead Sea Scrolls. Qumran in Perspective* (London, 1977) Collins), p. 46. Hereinafter: Vermes. All translations derive from G. Vermes, *The Dead Sea Scrolls in English* (Harmondsworth, 1975: Penguin Books, Ltd.). The Community Rule is on pp. 71-95, the Damascus Rule, pp. 95-118, the War Rule, pp. 122-149

Yet another rule, called the Damascus Rule, provides law on the organization of the institutions of the community, vows and oaths, the tribunal, witnesses and judges, purification by water, Sabbath observances, cultic cleanness, and the like. Still another, the War Rule, describes the conduct of a war to be fought at the end of time. In fact the war represents the struggle between good and evil, in which God will intervene. Vermes describes the document as follows: The author places the spiritual battle within an imaginary historical context and provides the armies of angels and demons with earthly allies: the Sons of Light are represented by the children of Levi, Judah, and Benjamin; the Sons of Darkness, by the Gentiles headed by the final enemy, the Kittim. Jerusalem is foreseen as reconquered after six years of the war, and the Temple worship restored, and plans for a defeat of all the foreign nations are elaborated in the seventh year. The Temple Scroll presents rules on purity and impurity, festivals, building the Temple, and the Israelite king and his army. There are in addition writings of hymns, psalms, prayers, and wisdom. In all, if we invoke once more the three principal strands of Scriptural writings, we find continuations of all three: Torah-writings of doctrine and law, prophetic-historical writings on the meaning and end of history, and sapiential writings on the correct conduct of everyday affairs.

The group represented by the writings that describe the way of life of a holy community preparing for a war at the end of time and the world-view of a struggle between light and darkness saw itself as Israel, pure and simple: the true Israel. The group divided up into priests and laity, with the priests called the sons of Zadok, recalling the legitimate high priest in the time of David. The lay people divided themselves into twelve tribes. So the whole meant to recapitulate, in the here and now, the true Israel of the scriptural account. A high point in the life of this "Israel" was its common meal:

That the common table was of high importance to Qumran daily life is evident from the fact that only the fully professed and the faultless....were allowed to sit at it. There is no explicit mention of a ritual bath preceding the meals, but from various references to purification by water...it is likely that the sectaries immersed themselves before eating.

Since in the priests' Torah, the consideration of cultic cleanness concerned the Temple in general, and in connection with eating food in particular, specifically, meals made up of the priests' share of the sacrifices to the Lord in the Temple, we may draw one inference. The "Israel" resident by the Dead Sea saw itself as a holy community bound by the rules governing the sanctification of the Temple priesthood in the conduct of those aspects of the life of that priesthood that pertained: eating holy meals. Vermes finds in the description of the group two distinct societies, one resident in the desert, the other in cities. In the former, the community lived in seclusion, in the latter, the members were surrounded by outsiders. But both groups claimed to constitute the true Israel. The sect lasted as a social group, a Judaism, from the beginning of the second century B.C. to A.D. 68, when the community was destroyed by the Romans. The end of the world indeed had come, and the Temple was destroyed shortly afterward.

The single characteristic trait of the Qumran Judaism was its emphasis on the community as the elect, united here and now with the angels of heaven:

> God has caused his chosen ones to inherit the lot of his holy ones.
> He has joined their assembly to the sons of heaven,
> to be a council of the community
> a foundation of the building of holiness
> an eternal plantation throughout all ages to come.

Each one who joined the group entered that remnant of Israel. Then all formed those "'sons of light" that would endure to the end:

> "Those born of truth spring from a fountain of light, but those born of falsehood spring from a source of darkness. All the children of righteousness are ruled by the Prince of Light and walk in the ways of light, but all the children of falsehood are ruled by the Angel of Darkness and walk in the ways of darkness.

In its own way, the community lived by its own rhythm, as the doctrine outlined here would lead us to expect. All commentators on the library of Qumran have found striking the community's sense of itself as different, separate from the rest of Israel, the clean few among the unclean many, the saved few, the children of light. The fundamental notion that the small group constituted in microcosm the Israel that mattered rests on the premise that the "Israel" out there, the nation as a whole, lives on condition and responds to stipulation. The "Israel" out there had failed; it is (in the mind of the Israel at hand) the children of darkness.

By "Israel" the authorships of the documents of the library of Qumran mean "us" — and no one else. We start with that "us" and proceed from there to "Israel," which turns out to be "us" and nobody else. The group's principal documents comprised a Community Rule, which "legislates for a kind of monastic society," the Damascus Rule, "for an ordinary lay existence," and the War Rule and Messianic Rule, "while associated with the other two, and no doubt reflecting to some extent a contemporary state of affairs, plan for a future age." Among the four, the first two will tell us their authorships' understanding of the relationship between "us" and "Israel," and that is what is critical to the picture of the type of "us" which (as we shall see) is "Israel" at hand. They structured their group — in Vermes's language, "so that it corresponded faithfully to that of Israel itself, dividing it into priests and laity, the priests being described as the 'sons of Zadok' — Zadok was High Priest in David's time — and the laity grouped after the biblical model into twelve tribes." This particular Israel then divided itself into units of thousands, hundreds, fifties, and tens. The Community Rule further knows divisions within the larger group, specifically, "the men of holiness," the men of perfect holiness," within a larger "Community." The corporate being of the community came to realization in common meals, prayers, and deliberations Vermes says, "Perfectly obedient to each and every one of the laws of Moses and to all that was commanded by the prophets, they were to love one another and to share with one another their knowledge, powers, and possessions."

The description of the inner life of the group presents us with a division of a larger society. But among many probative ones one detail tells us that this group implicitly conceived of itself as "Israel." At the center of the group's indicative traits is the simple fact that the group lived apart from the Temple of Jerusalem, deemed the existing temple null, and even had its liturgical life worked out in utter isolation from that central cult. They had their own calendar, which differed from the one people take for granted was observed in general, for their calendar was reckoned not by the moon but by the sun. This yielded different dates for the holy days and effectively marked the group as utterly out of touch with other Jews (and vice versa). The solar calendar followed by the community at Qumran meant that holy days for that group were working days for others and vice versa. The group furthermore had its own designation for various parts of the year. The year was divided into seven fifty-day periods, as Vermes says, each marked by an agricultural festival, e.g., the Feast of New Wine, Oil, and so on. On the Pentecost, treated as the Feast of the Renewal of the Covenant, the group would assembly in hierarchical order: "the priests first, ranked in order of status, after them the Levites, and lastly 'all the people one after another in their Thousands, Hundreds, Fifties, and Tens, that every Israelite may know his place in the community of God according to the everlasting design." There can be no doubt from this passage — and a vast array of counterparts can be assembled — that the documents at hand address "Israel." The priests' blessing of the "Israel" at hand corresponds, therefore, to the priestly blessing of Num. 6:24-26:

> May he bless you with all good and preserve you from all evil. May he lighten your heart with life-giving wisdom and grant you eternal knowledge. May he raise his merciful face toward you for everlasting bliss.
>
> Other rites, involving purification, the common meal, eaten in a state of cultic cleanness, and the like, suggest that we deal with an "Israel" that in its metaphorical thought about itself forms the counterpart to the holy Temple in Jerusalem, an "Israel" that, as a social group, constitutes the entirety of the "commu-

nity of Israel" in the here and now. Vermes makes this matter explicit:

> The Council of the Community was to be the 'Most Holy Dwelling of Aaron' where 'without the flesh of holocausts and the fat of sacrifice,' a 'sweet fragrance' was to be sent up to God, and where prayer was to serve 'as an acceptable fragrance of righteousness.'

It follows, as Vermes says, that "the Community [we should read: this "Israel"] itself was to be the sacrifice offered to God in atonement for Israel's sins." So much for a rapid description of components for the construction of a system as revealed by the documents at hand. We are not yet ready to reach an estimate of whether these components are so composed as to present a system. That judgment awaits the evidence of the second indicator, the logics of cogent discourse, at least, those characteristic of the more important writings.

Since what we have is not a systemic statement but a (mere) library of documents that exhibit (we take for granted) a certain affinity of viewpoint, we should also not expect that any uniformity of logic should characterize all of the writings. That proposition, on the surface, appears to invite a display of instantiation of banality. Why should we expect a diverse writers to appeal to a single logic of cogent discourse, other than one so general as to prove nothing of consequence. Accordingly, we focus upon only writing of precisely the same classification and ask whether, when proposing to say the same sort of things for the same purposes, the authorships before us adopt for their statements pretty much the same modes of intelligible exchange of thought. For that purpose, further, we wish to identify a kind of writing that in the original Judaic system, the Pentateuchal one, proved uniform in its appeal to a distinctive framing of a particular logic. These two conditions are met by passages that set forth laws. The problem facing the writers is the same, namely, how so to present rules of public conduct as to convey sense and meaning to the audience? Not only so, but the Pentateuchal logic of law-writing, briefly noted in the preceding chapter, proved entirely consistent and uniform. When the Pentateuchal authorship wished to compile and arrange facts/sentences involving normative conduct, it appealed throughout to teleological logic. That is the logic that set forth rules in a narrative context and thereby explained the sense and cogency of the rules in terms of that ultimate purpose gained by keeping those rules. So the way in which the shards and pieces of received materials were joined, which was through a fictive narrative with a beginning, middle, and end, also was the way in which the details of the law were sewn together into sustained statements, cogent within, coherent with the whole.

Now when we turn to the library found at Qumran, can we identify counterpart writings to the legal passages of the Pentateuch? Of course we can. And the problem is the same, since we have two distinct law codes, the Damascus Rule and the Community Rule, as well as yet another code, the War Rule. In the translation of Geza Vermes, these open, respectively, as follows: Damascus Rule:

> Hear now, all you who know righteousness and consider the works of God; for He has a dispute with all flesh and will condemn all those who despise Him.
> For when they were unfaithful and forsook Him, He hid His face from Israel and His sanctuary and delivered them up to the sword. But remembering the covenant of the forefathers He left a remnant to Israel and did not deliver it up to be destroyed. And in the age of wrath, three hundred and ninety years after He had given them into the hand of king Nebuchadnezzar of Babylon, He visited them, and He caused a plant root to spring from Israel and Aaron to inherit His land and to prosper on the good things of His earth. And they perceived their iniquity and recognized that they were guilty men, yet for twenty years they were blind men groping for the way.
> And God observed their deeds, that they sought him with a whole heart, and he raised for them a teacher of righteousness to guide them in the way of His heart. And he made known to the latter generations that which God had done to the latter generation, the congregation of traitors, to those who departed from the way....

Another sample passage of the Damascus Rule is as follows::

> None of the men who enter the New Covenant in the land of Damascus and who again betray it and depart from the fountain of living waters shall be reckoned with the Council of the people or inscribed in its Book from the day of the gathering in of the Teacher of the Community until the coming of the Messiah out of Aaron and Israel.

This is how the community rule starts:

> Community Rule:
> The master shall teach the saints to live according to the Book of the Community Rule, that they may seek God with a whole heart and soul and do what is good and right before Him as He commanded by the hand of Moses and all his servants the prophets; that they may love all that he has chosen and hate all that he has rejected; that they may abstain from all evil and hold fast to all god; that they may practice truth, righteousness, and justice upon earth and no longer stubbornly follow a sinful heart and lustful eyes, committing all manner of evil. He shall admit into the covenant of grace all those who have freely devoted themselves to the observance of God's precepts, that they may be joined to the counsel of God and may live perfectly before Him in accordance with all that has been revealed concerning their appointed times, and that they may love all the sons of light, each according to his lot in God's design, and hate all the sons of darkness, each according to his built in God's vengeance.

Other paragraphs from the Community Rule follow:

> No man shall walk in the stubbornness of his heart...but he shall circumcise in the Community the foreskin of evil inclination and of stiffness of neck, that they may lay a foundation of truth for Israel, for the Community of the everlasting Covenant. They shall atone for all those in Aaron who have freely pledged themselves to holiness, and for those in Israel who have freely pledged themselves to the House of Truth, and for those who join them to live in community and to take part in the trial and judgment and condemnation of all those who transgress the precepts.

But when a man enters the Covenant to walk according to all these precepts that he may join the holy congregation, they shall examine his spirit in community with respect to his understanding and practice of the Law, under the authority of the sons of Aaron who have freely pledged themselves in the Community to restore His covenant and to heed all the precepts commanded by Him, and of the multitude of Israel who have freely pledged themselves in the Community to return to his covenant...

When these become members of the Community in Israel according to all these rules, they shall establish the spirit of holiness according to everlasting truth...At that time the men of the Community shall set apart a House of Holiness in order that it may be united to the most holy things, and a House of Community for Israel, for those who walk in perfection...

The opening paragraphs of the War Rule follow:

War Rule:
For the Master. The Rule of War on the unleashing of the attack of the sons of light against the company of the sons of darkness, the army of Satan: against the band of Edom, Moab, and the sons of Ammon, and against the army of the sons of the East and the Philistines, and against the bands of the Kittim of Assyria and their allies the ungodly of the covenant.

The sons of Levi, Judah, and Benjamin, the exiles in the desert, shall battle against them in...all their bands when the exiled sons of light return from the Desert of the Peoples to camp in the Desert of Jerusalem; and after the battle they shall go up from there....

The king of the Kittim shall enter into Egypt and in his time he shall set out in great wrath to wage war against the kings of the north, that his fury may destroy and cut off the horn of...

There shall be a time of salvation for the people of God, an age of dominion for all the members of His company and of everlasting destruction for all the company of Satan. The confusion of the sons of Japheth shall be [great] and Assyria shall fall unsuccored. The dominion of the Kittim shall come to an end and iniquity shall be vanquished, leaving no remnant; for [the sons] of darkness there shall be no escape. [The seasons of righteous]ness shall shine over all the ends of the earth; they shall go on shining until all the seasons of darkness are con-

> sumed and, at the season appointed by God, His exalted greatness shall shine eternally to the peace, blessing, glory, joy, and long life of all the sons of light.
> On the day when the Kittim fall, there shall be battle and terrible carnage before the God of Israel, for that shall be the day appointed from ancient times for the battle of the destruction of the sons of darkness...

So much for some exemplary passages. I presented the three law-codes in the order that I chose because, reading them in this way, we see them as rules covering the beginning, middle, and end of the community, and perhaps that is how someone ordered them or understood their relationships. In a systemic document, at any rate, the three codes can have been presented within a single seamless statement, each with its span of applicability. But in a library, they set side by side, without any clear points of contact, let alone coherence, at all.

The Damascus Rule begins in such a way as to remind us of the intent of the compilers of Deuteronomy, which is to set the laws into a narrative setting. But there is no appeal to the end-time, such as dominates in Deuteronomy. The logic is not precisely the same as that of Deuteronomy, since, at the opening lines, the Damascus Rule's authorship seems to appeal to the past, not to the future, for the apologia for, and hence also the coherence of, the discrete rules that are to follow. But so far as the entries that make up the Rule are set forth as the statement of a way of life within the context of a world-view, it is by appeal to the origins of that "Israel," that remnant, that the laws govern. And in that general way, the rule does recall the logic of the Pentateuch. Such a rather general observation, standing by itself a mere banality, takes on consequence when we turn to the second and third law-codes, for each of them appeals to its own logic, and the logic of the one is not congruent to that of the other two. Consequently, the three writings do not lay claim to the same intellectual media for conveying intelligible meaning, in setting forth this fact, then that fact, and connecting the two.

The Community Rule tells us the purpose of the laws, and in

that sense, it too appeals to a teleological logic. But the purpose is not enveloped within a Deuteronomic historical account of the beginning, middle, and promised end of the social entity, the remnant of Israel that is Israel. The appeal now is to the everyday religious world of the community: "that they may seek God." At stake is holiness, the right attitude, living within the covenant, all in the context of admission to the community. The logic that joins one thing to the next, in my judgment, derives from that one point: the entry into the social entity. That centerpiece and keystone, holding the whole together, is not only original to the document, there being no counterpart interest in the large-scale statements of the Pentateuchal codes, seen whole or in their divisions. It also differs from the encompassing statement set forth by the Damascus Rule, which as we saw has a quite different focus of interest.

The War Rule tells the story of a war to be conducted in due course. But what holds the long list of rules together is not that story, but the concern correctly to lay out the armies and conduct the battle in accord with the law pertaining at the end of days. In telling how things are to be done at the end, the authorship at hand finds self-evidently related a variety of rather odd statements:

> On the trumpets calling the congregation they shall write, "The Called of God."
> On the trumpets calling the chiefs, they shall write, "The Princes of God."
> On the trumpets of the levies they shall write, "The Army of God...."
> When they march out to battle they shall write on their standards, Truth of God, Justice of God, Glory of God, Judgment of God, followed by the whole ordered list of their names.
> When they approach for battle they shall write on their standards, Right Hand of God, Appointed time of God, Tumult of God, Slain of God, followed by the whole list of their names.
> When they return from battle, they shall write on their standards, Honor of God, Majesty of God, Splendor of God, Glory of God, together with the whole list of their names.

And on and on. Clearly, these details spell out a large message, and a correct understanding of the layout, repetition, and order, will convey to the initiated a fundamental proposition, stated in one detail or another, throughout the document. The repetitious syntax and word-order, the highly formalized pattern, imparts to the treatment of a single subject a single and remarkably cogent style. In that way, the whole is holds together, and the parts also are made to match. Now, by contrast, a counterpart passage of the Damascus Rule:

> And this is the Rule for the Judges of the Congregation:
> Ten shall be elected from the congregation for a definite time, four from the tribe of Levi and Aaron, and six from Israel...No man over the age of sixty shall hold office as Judge of the Congregation, for "because man sinned his days have been shortened, and in the heat of his anger against the inhabitants of the earth God ordained that their understanding should depart even before their days are completed" (Jubilees 23:11).
> Concerning purification by water:
> No man shall bathe in dirty water or in an amount too shallow to cover a man. He shall not purify himself with water contained in a vessel. And as for the water of every rock-pool too shallow to cover a man, if an unclean man touches it, he renders its water as unclean as water contained in a vessel.
> Concerning the Sabbath to observe it according to its law:
> No man shall work on the sixth day from the moment when the sun's orb is distant by its own fullness from the gate (wherein it sinks)...No man shall speak any vain or idle word on the Sabbath day. He shall make no loan to his companion. He shall make no decision in matters of money and gain. He shall say nothing about work or labor to be done on the morrow.
> No man shall walk abroad to do business on the Sabbath. He shall not walk more than one thousand cubits beyond his town....

This seems to me a mere hodgepodge of this and that. For what joins these statements into a coherent unit? Certainly not that same subterranean, implicit principle expressed in detail only by the rules of the War Rule. I discern no effort at patterned language, a recurrent syntax, a repetition of word choices, for example. We have nothing more than a miscellany, this, that, the other thing, lacking all intrinsic connection deriving from proposition or other dimension of intent or meaning. We have an anthology of rules, not a coherent statement made through the topical order, rhetorical preferences, and propositional program alike. The contrast to the rigorous patterning of syntax and word-choice in the War Rule is blatant.

Any claim that a set of rules governing the life of the community is to be distinguished from an eschatological law-code governing the final battle is challenged by the literary and logical traits of the Community Rule. For the Community Rule, for its part, is far more carefully ordered than the Damascus Rule, indeed so different that we must wonder how a single authorship can have produced both documents, and its sequence of rules fit together, item by item, in an unfolding exposition of a coherent system. Whole and in its parts, it forms a well-constructed composition. Take for example the rule for a meeting:

> This is the rule for an assembly of the congregation:
> Each man shall sit in his place: the priest shall sit first, and the elders second, and all the rest of the people according to their rank. And thus they shall be questioned concerning the law, and concerning any counsel or matters coming before the Congregation, each man bringing his knowledge to the Council of the Community.
> No man shall interrupt a companion before his speech has ended nor speak before a man of higher rank; each man shall speak in his turn...
> Every man, born of Israel, who freely pledges himself to joint the Council of the Community, shall be examined by the Guardian at the head of the Congregation concerning his understanding and his deeds....

While a detailed survey of the document would prove tedious, perhaps another example, chosen more or less at random, of its remarkable adherence to a single logical program of exposition will prove of interest in making the main point. Here are five successive sentences:

> Whoever has deliberately lied shall do penance for six months.
> Whoever has deliberately insulted his companion unjustly shall

do penance for one year and shall be excluded. Whoever has deliberately deceived his companion by word or by deed shall do penance for six months.

We scarcely need to be informed that the passage bears its own superscription: "These are the rules by which they shall judge at a community (court of) inquiry according to the cases." In fact a patterned language, whoever has...shall do penance for..., in form links the statements. A single topic is discussed in that single pattern, namely, infringements by one party upon the rights and dignity of another. And of course the implicit principle, that each member of the community must respect the property and dignity of other members, is made self-evident in detail. The logic of coherent discourse, coming to formal expression in syntax and sentence-structure, finding a counterpart in the substantive principle that is expressed, attains perfection. Other documents exhibit their own patterns, or no patterns, but none links itself to any other.

The thread of my argument should not disappear in this mass of discrete observations about the literary and logical program of three authorships. We started by selecting, from the shelves of the library, three items of a single classification, construed as law-codes. We wanted to know whether three authorships invoked the same modes of intelligible exchange of thought, as to both logic and, in the nature of things, rhetoric as well. We now recognize that they do not. The three authorships' presentations of rules of public conduct convey sense and meaning, each in its own way. The question of whether or not in inner logic and in fundamental proposition the three documents cohere, as they do in temporal sequence of their topical programs, hardly requires much attention. Of the documents as a group we may say only that they represent messages evidently delivered to (or planned for) a single group, rather than different people talking about different things to different people. But that hardly presents us with a counterpart to the Pentateuchal system, and I think we now recognize that, when we enter into the heart of matters, we do not find at the library of Qumran the system and logical cogency that characterized the intellect of Judaism represented by the Pentateuch.

For what should we have located, in the writings at hand, to permit us to treat as taxonomically uniform the Pentateuchal and Qumran systems and their statements? For such a comparison and contrast, the Pentateuch by definition dictates the indicators. There we found, in the case of bits and pieces of diverse law-codes, single seamless voice, a sustained effort to string together this and that into a coherent and, so far as possible, cogent statement. A single logic, the teleological, joined this to that, turning facts into propositions and, consequently, sentences into paragraphs. The entire composite was made into an on-going and continuous composition, so that the world-view was set forth as the context for the required way of life, and so that the ethics and the ethos together joined to explain the identification of the social entity of the system as a whole, namely, Israel. Clearly, were we of a mind, we could ourselves compose a, or the, system of the "Israel" of Qumran. There is no single logic of cogent discourse, but diverse logics. There is no well composed account of the whole, merely bits and pieces of information that all together might form a whole. What is lacking in my view is not only a cogent logic and a manifest systemic statement, but a clear intent to draw together into a system, in some way we can now identify the shards and remnants of a system. But no such systemic statement derives from the library of Qumran, and nothing we have in hand suggests that any authorship undertook to compose the counterpart to the Pentateuchal statement and construct an equivalent to the Pentateuchal system.

Can we then describe the intellect of the Judaism of Qumran? I think not. The reason is that I do not know how to relate the system to its logic. As we have seen, the documents appeal, each to the logic that serves its authorship's purpose. The documents intersect but do not form a continuous statement. So by the two criteria that served us so well in our encounter with the Pentateuch, we have considerable difficulty in classifying the writings at hand as a system at all, hence in claiming also to describe the intellect that comes to expression in the shape and structure of that system. To state matters simply, we require of the Israel at Qumran two things. The first is a sustained and coherent account of the world-view of the group, the way of life to be lived by the group, the definition of the "Israel" constituted by the social entity at hand. The second is a cogent logic that serves to establish connections between one thing and something else and to guide us in drawing the correct conclusions from those connections. It goes without saying that showing the way in which the system dictates its logic, such as, overall, we are able to accomplish for the Pentateuchal Judaism, then presents us with a picture of the intellect that sees things one way, rather than some other, and so composes a worldview, a way of life an account of an "Israel," in this way, rather than that. Since we cannot correlate system and logic, we do not know, in the end, the layout of the intellect at hand, the interiority of the system if it was a system, of the library at Qumran. That alas, leaves us puzzled, which is precisely where, in literary form, the writings at hand are meant to leave us: certain as to the interrelationships of writings that are assuredly not autonomous of one another, even clear as to the connections, curious about the continuities, if any.

CHAPTER TWELVE

LIST-MAKING AND SYSTEM-BUILDING IN THE MISHNAH

The model of the intellect of the Pentateuch's system builders, successfully matching systemic statement to interior logic, in the contrast not only highlights the ambiguity of identifying the intellect of the Essene Judaism adumbrated by the collection of writings found at Qumran. It also helps us identify the intellect, and appreciate the remarkable success, of the authorship of the Mishnah. For in setting forth a system and identifying the logic required for its full interior structure, recognition of the achievement of the Pentateuchal Judaism helps us in the comparison also to discern the accomplishment of the Mishnah's framers in the document they produced in ca. A.D. 200. Alone among all exemplars of the intellect of Judaism in classical times, they point by point constructed their system just as did the Pentateuchal authorship.

The parallels are exact and complete. Just as the earlier compositors in ca. 450 B.C. had drawn upon received materials and laid them out in a manner of their own choosing, so did the Mishnah's authorship. Exactly as had the earlier writers set forth not a mélange of this and that but a well-composed and proportioned, (in context) seamless, and continuous statement, so too the Mishnah's framers presented to their "Israel" a proportioned, balanced, and fully exposed, closed system. Precisely as the Pentateuch's final compositors found a prevailing logic with which to sew together one thing to something else in an unbroken skein, so the Mishnah's ultimate authorship invoked a single logic throughout in the presentation of a tightly constructed structure, secure at all the joints of its frame. And just as the justifiably proud Pentateuchal compilers and writers then give the honor of authorship to God via the medium of Moses, so the authorship of the Mishnah present a free-standing document, with slight connection to any that had gone before, so that, within a generation, their heirs and apologists could assign origin of the whole to God's revelation of Torah, inclusive of orally formulated and orally transmitted tradition, to Moses at Sinai.

All the more surprising, therefore, that the Pentateuchal system and the Mishnaic system have virtually nothing in common. They exhibit shared preferences neither in form, nor in systemic statement and interest. Rhetorically, logically, and topically, they might as well have come down, each from its own planet to an utterly uncomprehending earth populated by the authorship of the other. The differences in language between biblical and Mishnaic or Middle Hebrew need not detain us and are, systemically, inert. But the differences in logic, perspective, and focus will demand our attention. For they are fundamental. The Pentateuch tells a story and weaves all rules into that story. Its logic is fundamentally teleological, and into that logic all its rules are fit. The Mishnah presents rules and treats stories (inclusive of history) as incidental and of merely taxonomic interest. Its logic is propositional, and its intellect does its work through a vast labor of classification, comparison, and contrast generating governing rules and generalizations. The Pentateuch provides an account of how things were in order to explain how things are and set forth how they should be, with the tabernacle in the wilderness the model for (and modeled after) the Temple in the Jerusalem building. The Mishnah speaks in a continuing present tense, saying only how things are, indifferent to the were and the will-be. The Pentateuch focuses upon self-conscious "Israel," saying who they were and what they must become to overcome how they now are. The Mishnah understands by "Israel" as much the individual as the nation and identifies as its principal actors, the heroes of its narrative, not the family become a nation, but the priest and the householder, the woman and the slave, the adult and the child, and other castes and categories of person within an inward-looking, established, fully landed community. Given the Mishnah's authorship's interest in classifications and categories, therefore in systematic hierarchization of an orderly world, one can hardly find odd that (re)definition of the subject-matter and problematic of the systemic social entity.

Let us dwell on this matter of difference in the prevailing logic. While the Pentateuch appeals to teleology to draw together and make sense of facts, so making connections by appeal to the end and drawing conclusions concerning the purpose of things, the Mishnah's authorship knows only the philosophical logic of syllogism, the rule-making logic of lists. The Pentateuchal logic reached concrete expression in narrative, which served to point to the direction and goal of matters, hence, in the nature of things, of history. Accordingly, those authors, when putting together diverse materials, so shaped everything as to form of it all as continuous a narrative as they could construct, and through that "history" that they made up, they delivered their message and also portrayed that message as cogent and compelling. If the Pentateuchal writers were theologians of history, the Mishnah's aimed at composing a natural philosophy for supernatural, holy Israel. Like good Aristotelians, they would uncover the components of the rules by comparison and contrast, showing the rule for one thing by finding out how it compared with like things and contrasted with the unlike.

Then, in their view, the unknown would become known, conforming to the rule of the like thing, also to the opposite of the rule governing the unlike thing.

That purpose is accomplished, in particular, though list-making, which places on display the data of the like and the unlike and implicitly (ordinarily, not explicitly) then conveys the role. That is why, in exposing the interior logic of its authorship's intellect, the Mishnah had to be a book of lists, with the implicit order, the nomothetic traits, dictating the ordinarily unstated general and encompassing rule. And all this why? It is in order to make a single statement, endless times over, and to repeat in a mass of tangled detail precisely the same fundamental judgment. The Mishnah in its way is as blatantly repetitious in its fundamental statement as is the Pentateuch. But the power of the Pentateuchal authorship, denied to that of the Mishnah, lies in their capacity always to be heard, to create sound by resonance of the surfaces of things. The Pentateuch is a fundamentally popular and accessible piece of writing. By contrast, the Mishnah's writers spoke into the depths, anticipating a more acute hearing than they ever would receive. So the repetitions of Scripture reinforce the message, while the endlessly repeated paradigm of the Mishnah sits too deep in the structure of the system to gain hearing from the ear that lacks acuity or to attain visibility to the untutored eye. So much for the logic. What of the systemic message? Given the subtlety of intellect of the Mishnah's authorship, we cannot find surprising that the message speaks not only in what is said, but in what is omitted.

When we listen to the silences of the system of the Mishnah, as much as to its points of stress, we hear a single message. It is a message of a system that answered a single encompassing question, and the question formed a stunning counterpart to that of the sixth century B.C. The Pentateuchal system addressed one reading of the events of the sixth century, highlighted by the destruction of the Jerusalem Temple in 586 B.C. At stake was how Israel as defined by that system related to its land, represented by its Temple, and the message may be simply stated: what appears to be the given is in fact a gift, subject to stipulations. The precipitating event for the Mishnaic system was the destruction of the Jerusalem Temple in A.D. 70, but at stake now was a quite fresh issue. It was, specifically, this: what, in the aftermath of the destruction of the holy place and holy cult, remained of the sanctity of the holy caste, the priesthood, the holy land, and, above all, the holy people and its holy way of life? The answer was that sanctity persists, indelibly, in Israel, the people, in its way of life, in its land, in its priesthood, in its food, in its mode of sustaining life, in its manner of procreating and so sustaining the nation. The Mishnah's system therefore focused upon the holiness of the life of Israel, the people, a holiness that had formerly centered on the Temple.

The logically consequent question was, what is the meaning of sanctity, and how shall Israel attain, or give evidence of, sanctification. The answer to the question derived from the original creation, the end of the Temple directing attention to the beginning of the natural world that the Temple had (and would again) embodied. For the meaning of sanctity the framers therefore turned to that first act of sanctification, the one in creation,. It came about when, all things in array, in place, each with its proper name, God blessed and sanctified the seventh day on the eve of the first Sabbath. Creation was made ready for the blessing and the sanctification when all things were very good, that is to say, in their rightful order, called by their rightful name. An orderly nature was a sanctified and blessed nature, so dictated Scripture in the name of the Supernatural. So to receive the blessing and to be made holy, all things in nature and society were to be set in right array. Given the condition of Israel, the people, in its land, in the aftermath of the catastrophic war against Rome led by Bar Kokhba in 132-135, putting things in order was no easy task. But that is why, after all, the question pressed, the answer proving inexorable and obvious. The condition of society corresponded to the critical question that obsessed the system-builders.

Once we discern that message, we shall also understand the logic necessary for its construction and inner structure. For the inner structure set forth by a logic of classification alone could sustain the system of ordering all things in proper place and under the proper rule. The like belongs with the like and conforms to the rule governing the like, the unlike goes over to the opposite and conforms to the opposite rule. When we make lists of the like, we also know the rule governing all the items on those lists, respectively. We know that and one other thing, namely, the opposite rule, governing all items sufficiently like to belong on those lists, but sufficiently unlike to be placed on other lists. That rigorously philosophical logic of analysis, comparison and contrast, served because it was the only logic that could serve a system that proposed to make the statement concerning order and right array that the Mishnah's authorship wished to set forth. To the urgent question, what of the holiness of Israel after the destruction of the Temple in A.D. 70, therefore, the system of the Mishnah provided the self-evidently valid answer and gave that answer in ineluctable and compelling logical form. That sanctification, as a matter of fact, from the viewpoint of the system now endured and transcended the physical destruction of the building and the cessation of sacrifices. For Israel the people was holy, enduring as the medium and the instrument of God's sanctification. The system then instructed Israel so to act as to express the holiness that inhered in the people. This Israel would accomplish by the right ordering, in accord with a single encompassing principle, of all details of the common life of the village and the home, matching the Temple and the cult.

In the Mishnaic Judaism do we deal with a tradition or a free-standing system? The Pentateuchal authorship, we recall, made ample and continuous use of received materials. So too the authorship of the Mishnah exploited what they chose, out of a heritage of facts deriving from we know not where, those facts it required for its structure and composition. Most of the Pentateuch derives from writers prior to the compilation and formation of the Pentateuch as we have it, but the Pentateuch is an utterly new composition. And what is new in the Mishnah is the system of the Mishnah, not most of the facts upon which the document draws. What the framers do with those facts gives the system its proportion and character, its systemic definition, power, message. For the framers ask their questions when they deal with a fairly broadly familiar corpus of facts. What defines the Mishnah's system is the generative questions the framers addressed to those facts, the trait or characteristic, about a given fact, that drew attention, made a difference and demanded emphasis. When we know what the authorship of the Mishnah wanted to know about a given subject and why that point of interest commanded attention, we define the generative problematic that made everything new in what was, as a matter of fact, a collection of commonplaces.

So we must appreciate the work of the authors of the document by appreciating the antiquity of many of the facts upon which they drew — beginning, after all, with Scripture itself. From Scripture onward, no other composition compares in size, comprehensive treatment of a vast variety of topics, balance, proportion, and cogency.

But the authors of the Mishnah reshaped whatever came into their hands. The document upon close reading proves systematic and orderly, purposive and well composed. Facts are formed into statements of sense and meaning, for the Mishnah is no mere scrapbook of legal data, arranged merely for purposes of reference. Each topic bears its point of interest, and that is what defines what the authorship wishes to tell us about that topic.

The Mishnah is a systemic document that is meant to make a statement on virtually every page, a document in which the critical problematic at the center almost always exercises influence over the merely instrumental, peripheral facts, dictating how they are chosen, arranged, utilized. So even though facts in the document prove very old indeed, on that basis we understand no more than we did before we knew that some of the document's data come from ancient times. True, law as the Mishnah presents law derives from diverse sources, from remote antiquity onward. But the law as it emerges whole and complete in the Mishnah, in particular, that is, the system, the structure, the proportions and composition, the topical program and the logical and syllogistic whole — these derive from the imagination and wit of the final two generations, of the authors of the Mishnah, that is, from ca. 140 to ca. 200. And through them the authorship delivers its message, asking its question by answering it again and again. But this answer comes only in picayune detail, as though the main issue were settled and beyond dispute, a remarkably powerful way of making one's main point.

Let me now spell out in some detail the basic statement that the document wishes to make. The Mishnah's system as a whole may be characterized in a simple way. Overall, its stress lies, as I said, on sanctification, understood as the correct arrangement of all things, each in its proper category, each called by its rightful name, just as at the creation. Then everything having been given its proper name, God called the natural world very good and therefore blessed and sanctified it. This stress on proper order and right rule explains why the Mishnah makes a statement of philosophy, concerning the order of the natural world in its correspondence with the supernatural world. The system of philosophy expressed through concrete and detailed law presented by the Mishnah, consists of a coherent logic and topic, a cogent world-view and comprehensive way of living. It is a world-view which speaks of transcendent things, a way of life in response to the supernatural meaning of what is done, a heightened and deepened perception of the sanctification of Israel in deed and in deliberation. Sanctification thus means two things, first, distinguishing Israel in all its dimensions from the world in all its ways; second, establishing the stability, order, regularity, predictability, and reliability of Israel in the world of nature and supernature in particular at moments and in contexts of danger. Danger means instability, disorder, irregularity, uncertainty, and betrayal. Each topic of the system as a whole takes up a critical and indispensable moment or context of social being. Through what is said in regard to each of the Mishnah's principal topics, what the system expressed through normative rules as a whole wishes to declare is fully expressed. Yet if the parts severally and jointly give the message of the whole, the whole cannot exist without all of the parts, so well joined and carefully crafted are they all.

As we attended in brief to the topical system of the Essene library of Qumran, so let us rapidly review the topical program of the Mishnah's system. The final statement of the Mishnah was divided into six principal topics, called in Hebrew seder [plural: sedarim] and in English divisions. To understand the complete system, we review these divisions as they were finally spelled out. The Division of Agriculture treats two topics, first, producing crops in accord with the scriptural rules on the subject, second, paying the required offerings and tithes to the priests, Levites, and poor. The principal point of the Division is that the Land is holy, because God has a claim both on it and upon what it produces. God's claim must be honored by setting aside a portion of the produce for those for whom God has designated it. God's ownership must be acknowledged by observing the rules God has laid down for use of the Land.

The Division of Appointed Times forms a system in which the advent of a holy day, like the Sabbath of creation, sanctifies the life of the Israelite village through imposing on the village rules on the model of those of the Temple. The purpose of the system, therefore, is to bring into alignment the moment of sanctification of the village and the life of the home with the moment of sanctification of the Temple on those same occasions of appointed times. The underlying and generative logic of the system comes to expression in a concrete way here. We recall the rule of like and opposite, comparison and contrast. What is not like something follows the rule opposite to that pertaining to that something. Here, therefore, since the village is the mirror image of the Temple, the upshot is dictated by the analogical-contrastive logic of the system as a whole. If things are done in one way in the Temple, they will be done in the opposite way in the village. Together the village and the Temple on the occasion of the holy day therefore form a single continuum, a completed creation, thus awaiting sanctification. The village is made like the Temple in that on appointed times one may not freely cross the lines distinguishing the village from the rest of the world, just as one may not freely cross the lines distinguishing the Temple from the world. But the village is a mirror image of the Temple. The boundary lines prevent free entry into the Temple, so they restrict free egress from the village. On the holy day what one may do in the Temple is precisely what one may not do in the village.

So the advent of the holy day affects the village by bringing it into sacred symmetry in such wise as to effect a system of opposites; each is holy, in a way precisely the opposite of the other. Because of the underlying conception of perfection attained through the union of opposites, the village is not represented as conforming to the model of the cult, but of constituting its antithesis. The world thus regains perfection when on the holy day heaven and earth are united, the whole completed and done: the heaven, the earth, and all their hosts. This moment of perfection renders the events of ordinary time, of "history," essentially irrelevant. For what really matters in time is that moment in which sacred time intervenes and effects the perfection formed of the union of heaven and earth, of Temple, in the model of the former, and Israel, its complement. It is not a return to a perfect time but a recovery of perfect being, a fulfillment of creation, which explains the essentially ahistorical character of the Mishnah's Division on Appointed Times. Sanctification constitutes an ontological category and is effected by the creator.

This explains why the division in its rich detail is composed of two quite distinct sets of materials. First, it addresses what one does in the sacred space of the Temple on the occasion of sacred time, as distinct from what one does in that same sacred space on ordinary, undifferentiated days, which is a subject worked out in Holy Things. Second, the Division defines how for the occasion of the holy day one creates a corresponding space in one's own circumstance, and what one does, within that space, during sacred time. The division as a whole holds together through a shared, generative metaphor. It is, as I said, the comparison, in the context of sacred time, of the spatial life of the Temple to the spatial life of the village, with activities and restrictions to be specified for each, upon the common occasion of the Sabbath or festival. The Mishnah's purpose therefore is to correlate the sanctity of the Temple, as defined by the holy day, with the restrictions of space and of action which make the life of the village different and holy, as defined by the holy day.

The Division of Women defines the women in the social economy of Israel's supernatural and natural reality. Women acquire definition wholly in relationship to men, who impart form to the Israelite social economy. The status of women is effected through both supernatural and natural, this-worldly action. What man and woman do on earth provokes a response in heaven, and the correspondences are perfect. So women are defined and secured both in heaven and here on earth, and that position is always and invariably relative to men. The principal interest for the Mishnah is the point at which a woman becomes, and ceases to be, holy to a particular man, that is, enters and leaves the marital union. These transfers of women are the dangerous and disorderly points in the relationship of woman to man, therefore, the Mishnah states, to society as well. The division's systemic statement stresses the preservation of order in transactions involving women and (other) property. Within this orderly world of documentary and procedural concerns a place is made for the disorderly conception of the marriage not formed by human volition but decreed in heaven, the levirate connection. Mishnah-tractate Yebamot states that supernature sanctifies a woman to a man (under the conditions of the levirate connection). What it says by indirection is that man sanctifies too: man, like God, can sanctify that relationship between a man and a woman, and can also effect the cessation of the sanctity of that same relationship. Five of the seven tractates of the Division of Women are devoted to the formation and dissolution of the marital bond. Of them, three treat what is done by man here on earth, that is, formation of a marital bond through betrothal and marriage contract and dissolution through divorce and its consequences. The Division and its system therefore delineate the natural and supernatural character of the woman's role in the social economy framed by man: the beginning, end, and middle of the relationship. The whole constitutes a significant part of the Mishnah's encompassing system of sanctification, for the reason that heaven confirms what men do on earth. A correctly prepared writ of divorce on earth changes the status of the woman to whom it is given, so that in heaven she is available for sanctification to some other man, while, without that same writ, in heaven's view, should she go to some other man, she would be liable to be put to death. The earthly deed and the heavenly perspective correlate. That is indeed very much part of larger system, which says the same thing over and over again.

 The Division of Damages comprises two subsystems, which fit together in a logical way. One part presents rules for the normal conduct of civil society. These cover commerce, trade, real estate, and other matters of everyday intercourse, as well as mishaps, such as damages by chattels and persons, fraud, overcharge, interest, and the like, in that same context of everyday social life. The other part describes the institutions governing the normal conduct of civil society, that is, courts of administration, and the penalties at the disposal of the government for the enforcement of the law. The two subjects form a single tight and systematic dissertation on the nature of Israelite society and its economic, social, and political relationships, as the Mishnah envisages them. The main point of the first of the two parts of the Division is that the task of society is to maintain perfect stasis, to preserve the prevailing situation, and to secure the stability of all relationships. To this end, in the interchanges of buying and selling, giving and taking, borrowing and lending, it is important that there be an essential equality of interchange. No party in the end should have more than what he had at the outset, and none should be the victim of a sizable shift in fortune and circumstance. All parties' rights to, and in, this stable and unchanging economy of society are to be preserved. When the condition of a person is violated, so far as possible the law will secure the restoration of the antecedent status.

The goal of the system of civil law is the recovery of the prevailing order and balance, the preservation of the established wholeness of the social economy. This idea is powerfully expressed in the organization of the three tractates that comprise the civil law, which treat first abnormal and then normal transactions. The framers deal with damages done by chattels and by human beings, thefts and other sorts of malfeasance against the property of others. The civil law in both aspects pays closest attention to how the property and person of the injured party so far as possible are restored to their prior condition, that is, a state of normality. So attention to torts focuses upon penalties paid by the malefactor to the victim, rather than upon penalties inflicted by the court on the malefactor for what he has done. When speaking of damages, the Mishnah thus takes as its principal concern the restoration of the fortune of victims of assault or robbery. Then the framers take up the complementary and corresponding set of topics, the regulation of normal transactions. When we rapidly survey the kinds of transactions of special interest, we see from the topics selected for discussion what we have already uncovered in the deepest structure of organization and articulation of the basic theme. The other half of this same unit of three tractates presents laws governing normal and routine transactions, many of them of the same sort as those dealt with in the first half. Bailments, for example, occur in both wings of the triple tractate, first, bailments subjected to misappropriation, or accusation thereof, by the bailiff, then, bailments transacted under normal circumstances. Under the rubric of routine transactions are those of workers and householders, that is, the purchase and sale of labor; rentals and bailments; real estate transactions; and inheritances and estates. Of the lot, the one involving real estate transactions is the most fully articulated and covers the widest range of problems and topics. The three tractates of the civil law all together thus provide a complete account of the orderly governance of balanced transactions and unchanging civil relationships within Israelite society under ordinary conditions.

The character and interests of the Division of Damages present probative evidence of the larger program of the philosophers of the Mishnah. Their intention is to create nothing less than a full-scale Israelite government, subject to the administration of sages. This government is fully supplied with a constitution and bylaws. It makes provision for a court system and procedures, as well as a full set of laws governing civil society and criminal justice. This government, moreover, mediates between its own community and the outside ("pagan") world. Through its system of laws it expresses its judgment of the others and at the same time defines, protects, and defends its own society and social frontiers. It even makes provision for procedures of remission, to expiate its own errors. The (then non-existent) Israelite government imagined by the second-century philosophers centers upon the (then non-existent) Temple, and the (then forbidden) city, Jerusalem. For the Temple is one principal focus. There the highest court is in session; there the high priest reigns. The penalties for law infringement are of three kinds, one of which involves sacrifice in the Temple. (The others are compensation, physical punishment, and death.) The basic conception of punishment, moreover, is that unintentional infringement of the rules of society, whether "religious" or otherwise, is not penalized but rather expiated through an offering in the Temple. If a member of the people of Israel intentionally infringes against the law, to be sure, that one must be removed from society and is put to death. And if there is a claim of one member of the people against another, that must be righted, so that the prior, prevailing status may be restored. So offerings in the Temple are given up to appease heaven and restore a whole bond between heaven and Israel, specifically on those occasions on which without malice or ill will an Israelite has disturbed the relationship. Israelite civil society without a Temple is not stable or normal, and not to be imagined. And the Mishnah is above all an act of imagination in defiance of reality.

The plan for the government involves a clear-cut philosophy of society, a philosophy which defines the purpose of the government and ensures that its task is not merely to perpetuate its own power. What the Israelite government, within the Mishnaic fantasy, is supposed to do is to preserve that state of perfection which, within the same fantasy, the society to begin everywhere attains and expresses. This is in at least five aspects. First of all, one of the ongoing principles of the law, expressed in one tractate after another, is that people are to follow and maintain the prevailing practice of their locale. Second, the purpose of civil penalties, as we have noted, is to restore the injured party to his prior condition, so far as this is possible, rather than merely to penalize the aggressor. Third, there is the conception of true value, meaning that a given object has an intrinsic worth, which, in the course of a transaction, must be paid. In this way the seller does not leave the transaction any richer than when he entered it, or the buyer any poorer (parallel to penalties for damages). Fourth, there can be no usury, a biblical prohibition adopted and vastly enriched in the Mishnaic thought, for money ("coins") is what it is. Any pretense that it has become more than what it was violates, in its way, the conception of true value. Fifth, when real estate is divided, it must be done with full attention to the rights of all concerned, so that, once more, one party does not gain at the expense of the other. In these and many other aspects the law expresses its obsession with the perfect stasis of Israelite society. Its paramount purpose is in preserving and ensuring that that perfection of the division of this world is kept inviolate or restored to its true status when violated.

The Division of Holy Things presents a system of sacrifice and sanctuary. The division centers upon the everyday and rules always applicable to the cult: the daily whole offering, the sin offering and guilt-offering which one may bring any time under ordinary circumstances; the right sequence of diverse offerings; the way in which the rites of the whole, sin-, and guilt-offerings are carried out; what sorts of animals are acceptable; the accompanying cereal offerings; the support and provision of animals for the cult and of meat for the priesthood; the support and material maintenance of the cult and its building. We have a system before us: the system of the cult of the Jerusalem Temple, seen as an ordinary and everyday affair, a continuing and routine operation. That is why special rules for the cult, both in respect to the altar and in regard to the maintenance of the buildings, personnel, and even the hold city, will be elsewhere — in Appointed Times and Agriculture. But from the perspective of Holy Things, those divisions intersect by supplying special rules and raising extraordinary (Agriculture: land bound; Appointed Times: time-bound) considerations for that theme which Holy Things claims to set forth in its most general and unexceptional way: the cult as something permanent and everyday.

The Division of Purities presents a very simple system of three principal parts: sources of uncleanness, objects and substances susceptible to uncleanness, and modes of purification from uncleanness. So it tells the story of what makes a given sort of object unclean and what makes it clean. Viewed as a whole, the Division of Purities treats the interplay of persons, food, and liquids. Dry inanimate objects or food are not susceptible to uncleanness. What is wet is susceptible. So liquids activate the system. What is unclean, moreover, emerges from uncleanness through the operation of liquids, specifically, through immersion in fit water of requisite volume and in natural condition. Liquids thus deactivate the system. Thus, water in its natural condition is what concludes the process by removing uncleanness. Water in its unnatural condition, that is, deliberately affected by human agency, is what imparts susceptibility to uncleanness to begin with. The uncleanness of persons, furthermore, is signified by body liquids or flux in the case of the menstruating woman and the zab (Lev. 15:1ff.). Corpse uncleanness is conceived to be a kind of effluent, a viscous gas, which flows like liquid. Utensils for their part receive uncleanness when they form receptacles able to contain liquid. In sum, we have a system in which the invisible flow of fluidlike substances or powers serve to put food, drink, and receptacles into the status of uncleanness and to remove those things from that status. Whether or not we call the system "metaphysical," it certainly has no material base but is conditioned upon highly abstract notions. Thus in material terms, the effect of liquid is upon food, drink, utensils, and man. The consequence has to do with who may eat and drink what food and liquid, and what food and drink may be consumed in which pots and pans. These loci are specified by tractates on utensils and on food and drink.

The human being is ambivalent. Persons fall in the middle, between sources and loci of uncleanness, because they are both. They serve as sources of uncleanness. They also become unclean. The zab, suffering the uncleanness described in Leviticus Chapter 15, the menstruating woman, the woman after childbirth, and the person afflicted with the skin ailment described in Leviticus Chapters 13 and 14 — all are sources of uncleanness. But being unclean, they fall within the system's loci, its program of consequences. So they make other things unclean and are subject to penalties because they are unclean. Unambiguous sources of uncleanness never also constitute loci affected by uncleanness. They always are unclean and never can become clean: the corpse, the dead creeping thing, and things like them. Inanimate sources of uncleanness and inanimate objects are affected by uncleanness. Systemically unique, man and liquids have the capacity to inaugurate the processes of uncleanness (as sources) and also are subject to those same processes (as objects of uncleanness).

The diverse topical program of the Mishnah, time and again

making the same points on the centrality of order, works itself out in a single logic of cogent discourse, one which seeks the rule that governs diverse cases. And, as we now see, that logic states within its interior structure the fundamental point of the document as a whole. The correspondence of logic to system here, as in the Pentateuch viewed overall, hardly presents surprises. Seeing how the logic does its work within the document therefore need not detain us for very long. Let us take up two pericopes of the Mishnah and determine the logic that joins fact to fact, sentence to sentence, in a cogent proposition, that is, in our terms, a paragraph that makes a statement. To see how this intellect does its work we turn first to Mishnah-tractate Berakhot, Chapter Eight, to see list-making in its simplest form, and then to Mishnah-tractate Sanhedrin, Chapter Two, to see the more subtle way in which list-making yields a powerfully argued philosophical theorem.

In the first of our two abstracts we have a list, carefully formulated, in which the announcement at the outset tells us what is catalogued, and in which careful mnemonic devices so arrange matters that we may readily remember the conflicting opinions. So in formal terms, we have a list that means to facilitate memorization. But in substantive terms, the purpose of the list and its message(s) are not set forth, and only ample exegesis will succeed in spelling out what is at stake. Here is an instance of a Mishnah-passage which demands an exegesis not supplied by the Mishnah's authorship.

Mishnah-tractate Berakhot Chapter Eight
8:1

[1]

A. These are the things which are between the House of Shammai and the House of Hillel in [regard to] the meal:

B. The House of Shammai say, "One blesses over the day, and afterward one blesses over the wine."

And the House of Hillel say, "One blesses over the wine, and afterward one blesses over the day."

8:2

[2] A. The House of Shammai say, "They wash the hands and afterward mix the cup."

And the House of Hillel say, "They mix the cup and after-

8:3

[3] A. The House of Shammai say, "He dries his hands on the cloth and lays it on the table."
And the House of Hillel say, "On the pillow."

8:4

[4] A. The House of Shammai say, "They clean the house, and afterward they wash the hands."
And the House of Hillel say, "They wash the hands, and afterward they clean the house."

8:5

[5] A. The House of Shammai say, "Light, and food, and spices, and habdalah."
And the House of Hillel say, "'Light, and spices, and food, and Habdalah."

[6] B. The House of Shammai say, "'Who created the light of the fire.'"
And the House of Hillel say, "'Who creates the lights of the fire.'"

The mnemonic serving the list does its work by the simple reversal of items. If authority A has the order 1, 2, then authority be will give 2, 1. Only entry [3] breaks that pattern. What is at stake in the making of the list is hardly transparent, and why day/wine vs. wine/day, with a parallel, e.g., clean/wash vs. wash/clean, yields a general principle the authorship does not indicate. All we know at this point, therefore, is that we deal with list-makers. But how lists work to communicate principles awaits exemplification.

The next abstract allows us much more explicitly to identify the and and the equal of Mishnaic discourse, showing us through the making of connections and the drawing of conclusions the propositional and essentially philosophical mind that animates the Mishnah. In the following passage, drawn from Mishnah-tractate Sanhedrin Chapter Two, the authorship wishes to say that Israel has two heads, one of state, the other of cult, the king and the high priest, respectively, and that these two offices are nearly wholly congruent with one another, with a few differences based on the particular traits of each. Broadly speaking, therefore, our exercise is one of setting forth the genus and the species. The genus is head of holy Israel. The species

Rabbinic Judaism's Generative Logic: Volume Two 79

are king and high priest. Here are the traits in common and those not shared, and the exercise is fully exposed for what it is, an inquiry into the rules that govern, the points of regularity and order, in this minor matter, of political structure. My outline, imposed in italic type, makes the point important in this setting.

Mishnah-tractate Sanhedrin Chapter Two
    1. *The rules of the high priest: subject to the law, marital rites, conduct in bereavement*

2:1
- A. A high priest judges, and [others] judge him;
- B. gives testimony, and [others] give testimony about him;
- C. performs the rite of removing the shoe [Deut. 25:7-9], and [others] perform the rite of removing the shoe with his wife.
- D. [Others] enter levirate marriage with his wife, but he does not enter into levirate marriage,
- E. because he is prohibited to marry a widow.
- F. [If] he suffers a death [in his family], he does not follow the bier.
- G. "But when [the bearers of the bier] are not visible, he is visible; when they are visible, he is not.
- H. "And he goes with them to the city gate," the words of R. Meir.
- I. R. Judah says, "He never leaves the sanctuary,
- J. "since it says, 'Nor shall he go out of the sanctuary' FO3 () (Lev. 21:12)."
- K. And when he gives comfort to others
- L. the accepted practice is for all the people to pass one after another, and the appointed [prefect of the priests] stands between him and the people.
- M. And when he receives consolation from others,
- N. all the people say to him, "Let us be your atonement."
- O. And he says to them, "May you be blessed by Heaven."
- P. And when they provide him with the funeral meal,
- Q. all the people sit on the ground, while he sits on a stool.

    2. *The rules of the king; not subject to the law, marital rites, conduct in bereavement*

2:2
- A. The king does not judge, and [others] do not judge him;
- B. does not give testimony, and [others] do not give testi-

mony about him;

C. does not perform the rite of removing the shoe, and others do not perform the rite of removing the shoe with his wife;

D. does not enter into levirate marriage, nor [do his brother] enter levirate marriage with his wife.

E. R. Judah says, "If he wanted to perform the rite of removing the shoe or to enter into levirate marriage, his memory is a blessing."

F. They said to him, "They pay no attention to him [if he expressed the wish to do so]."

G. [Others] do not marry his widow.

H. R. Judah says, "A king may marry the widow of a king.

I. "For so we find in the case of David, that he married the widow of Saul,

J. "For it is said, 'And I gave you your master's house and your master's wives into your embrace'

FO3()(2 Sam. 12:8)."

2:3

A. [If] [the king] suffers a death in his family, he does not leave the gate of his palace.

B. R. Judah says, "If he wants to go out after the bier, he goes out,

C. "for thus we find in the case of David, that he went out after the bier of Abner,

D. "since it is said, 'And King David followed the bier'

FO2()(2 Sam. 3:31)."

E. They said to him, "This action was only to appease the people."

F. And when they provide him with the funeral meal, all the people sit on the ground, while he sits on a couch.

3. Special rules pertinent to the king because of his calling

2:4

A. [The king] calls out [the army to wage] a war fought by choice on the instructions of a court of seventy-one.

B. He [may exercise the right to] open a road for himself, and [others] may not stop him.

C. The royal road has no required measure.

D. All the people plunder and lay before him [what they have grabbed], and he takes the first portion.

E. "He should not multiply wives to himself" (Deut. 17:17) — only eighteen.

F. R Judah says, "He may have as many as he wants, so long as they do not entice him [to abandon the Lord (Deut. 7:4)]."
G. R. Simeon says, "Even if there is only one who entices him [to abandon the Lord] — lo, this one should not marry her."
H. If so, why is it said, "He should not multiply wives to himself"?
I. Even though they should be like Abigail [1 Sam. 25:3].
J. "He should not multiply horses to himself" (Deut. 17:16) — only enough for his chariot.
K. "Neither shall he greatly multiply to himself silver and gold" (Deut. 17:16) — only enough to pay his army.
L. "And he writes out a scroll of the Torah for himself" (Deut. 17:17)
M. When he goes to war, he takes it out with him; when he comes back, he brings it back with him; when he is in session in court, it is with him; when he is reclining, it is before him,
N. as it is said, "And it shall be with him, and he shall read in it all the days of his life" (Deut. 17:19).

2:5
A. [Others may] not ride on his horse, sit on his throne, handle his scepter.
B. And [others may] not watch him while he is getting a haircut, or while he is nude, or in the bath-house,
C. since it is said, "You shall surely set him as king over you" (Deut. 17:15) — that reverence for him will be upon you.

The philosophical cast of mind is amply revealed in this essay, which in concrete terms effects a taxonomy, a study of the genus, national leader, and its two species, [1] king, [2] high priest: how are they alike, how are they not alike, and what accounts for the differences. The premise is that national leaders are alike and follow the same rule, except where they differ and follow the opposite rule from one another. But that premise also is subject to the proof effected by the survey of the data consisting of concrete rules, those systemically inert facts that here come to life for the purposes of establishing a proposition. By itself, the fact that, e.g., others may not ride on his horse, bears the burden of no systemic proposition. In the context of an argument constructed for nomothetic, taxonomic purposes, the same fact is active and weighty.

No natural historian can find the discourse and mode of thought at hand unfamiliar; it forms the foundation of all disposition of data in quest of meaning, in the language of Chapter Two of this book, making connections, drawing conclusions. For if I had to specify a single mode of thought that established connections between one fact and another, it is in the search for points in common and therefore also points of contrast. We seek connection between fact and fact, sentence and sentence in the subtle and balanced rhetoric of the Mishnah, by comparing and contrasting two things that are like and not alike. At the logical level, too, the Mishnah falls into the category of familiar philosophical thought. Once we seek regularities, we propose rules. What is like another thing falls under its rule, and what is not like the other falls under the opposite rule. Accordingly, as to the species of the genus, so far as they are alike, they share the same rule. So far as they are not alike, each follows a rule contrary to that governing the other. So the work of analysis is what produces connection, and therefore the drawing of conclusions derives from comparison and contrast: the and, the equal. The proposition then that forms the conclusion concerns the essential likeness of the two offices, except where they are different, but the subterranean premise is that we can explain both likeness and difference by appeal to a principle of fundamental order and unity. To make these observations concrete, we turn to the case at hand. The important contrast comes at the outset. The high priest and king fall into a single genus, but speciation, based on traits particular to the king, then distinguishes the one from the other. In a treatise on government, organizing details into unifying rules, the propositions of the present passage will have been stated differently. But the mode of thought, the manner of reaching conclusions, above all, the point I stressed so heavily in the first three chapters, the mind-set that sees connections in one way, rather than some other, that draws conclusions in this wise, not in that — these will have found an equally familiar place in the mind of both philosophy, of Aristotle's kind in particular, and the intellect of Judaism represented by the Mishnah.

But comparing the intellect of the Mishnah's system-builders to that of Aristotle diverts our gaze from the still more apt likeness, the one with which we commenced. Like the authorship of the Pentateuch, the framers of the Mishnah have drawn together diverse materials in a single, nearly-seamless fabric. And in them they have made a single statement, many times over, in the setting of an extraordinarily vast range of topics. Once authorship has registered the statement it wishes to make, it finds possible the expression of that same statement through what seems to me an unlimited range of topical media. Not only so, but just as in the Pentateuch a single logic of cogent discourse joins fact to fact and sentence to sentence into proposition and paragraph respectively, the same takes place in the Mishnah. That logic of list-making, which brings to the surface a deeper intellectual structure formed of comparison and contrast, classification and exclusion, predominates throughout. Accordingly, a single logic serves to make a single statement, in behalf of both the authorship of the Pentateuch and the framers of the Mishnah.

Speaking anonymously, collectively, and authoritatively, each set of system-builders has followed precisely the same rules of intellect, which, stated very simply, require a logic of a single taxon to make a statement. of a singular character. And, as in the Pentateuch, so in the Mishnah, the form of the logic must fit the framework of the statement: teleology for a statement made up of connections between events and lessons drawn from events, philosophical syllogism for a statement made up of rules governing (or deriving from) a variety of cases. And that brings us to the final issue of systemic analysis in quest of insight into intellect: both authorships leave open the question of tradition, since, as we see with great clarity, each group of system-builders has chosen to do one thing only: set forth a system, without laying claim to the authority of tradition. And that is surely a trait of intellect of system-builders, so persuaded of the compelling character of their statement as to deny need to invoke the authority of tradition. Logic takes the place of tradition, argument and powerful rhetoric, of the argument of precedent and an authoritative past. It is one thing to claim God said it all to Moses, who wrote it down. It is another to say that the unbroken chain of tradition from Sinai stands behind the document, and the Pentateuchal Judaism affirms the one and rejects the other. The Pentateuchal compositors claimed their system came not through tradition but from Sinai, dictated whole and complete by God to Moses. Given their extraordinary achievement, as I said, we need hardly find surprising the claim that, with enormous but entirely ordinate pride, they made in behalf of that achievement.

But the Mishnah's authorship claimed no less. For, in the very face of the Torah of God revealed to Moses at Sinai, they built and set forth a system resting wholly on the foundations of logic and order set forth within the systemic statement itself. That is to say, theirs was a statement standing on the firm two feet of the systemic authorship itself. The authorship of the Pentateuch appealed to Sinai for authority. The framers of the Mishnah kept silent about why people should keep the rules of their document and so construct out of an inchoate and chaotic world that system that they set forth. The systemic statement contained its own authority. That, at any rate, is what they seem to me implicitly to have said through those inviting silences that invite us, in the end, to join in the conversation they inaugurated. Logic, compelling and uncompromising, sustained the system; an appeal to tradition would have contradicted that proud claim of the system-makers of the Mishnah, and it is a claim that they did not deign to put forth. True, others alleged in their behalf that their authority, if not their exact positions, set them into a chain of tradition commencing with Moses at Sinai. But that claim came only in the context of debates following the closure of the Mishnah and made necessary by the character of the Mishnah. To state the upshot simply, the framers of the Mishnah set forth a system that, in its very nature, demanded to be transformed into a tradition. And that demand would rapidly be met by the authorship of the Bavli, but there too, in terms defined by that authorship, and for purposes dictated not by tradition but by yet another system-making intellect of Judaism, the last and best of classical times.

We shall now see that the intellectual labor of relating system to tradition and also of finding an appropriate logic of cogent discourse for the composition of a system could be accomplished in more than one way. A systemic statement could be woven into the cloak of tradition by its presentation as (mere) exegesis of a received text. The urgent question and self-evidently valid answer, not stated openly as a proposition for demonstration and argument, but merely repeated endlessly in the form of commentary, bore its own power of persuasion. Repeating the point gains for the message a self-evident that argument and therefore counterargument can deny it. And that brings us to the case of the Bavli, which shows that a systematic and philosophical statement may be set forth not only through a single, seamless composition, bearing a paramount logic, such as the Pentateuch or the Mishnah. It also could accomplish the same goal of order and proportion and persuasion even when comprising two or more logics on the one side, and even when not formed into a single seamless statement on the other. We remember that the manner of making connections and drawing conclusions, after all, does not percolate upward into the framing of the systemic statement, stage by stage. It is the system that defines its question and answer, and then, and only then, also chooses the logics required to effect the kind of discourse that the system-builders have chosen for their own purposes to undertake. But in some way, and through some well-reflected-upon mode of discourse, the system the builders wish to construct must ultimately reach fulfillment in systematic and philosophical statements. And in some way, these must be so constructed as to begin in first principles and to rise in steady and inexorable logic to final conclusions: compositions of proportion, balance, order, and, by the way, also cogency. So that brings us to the next and final phase in the formation of the intellect of Judaism. Onward to that chapter of the story.

CHAPTER THIRTEEN

THE MIXED LOGICS OF CONCLUSION AND CONNECTION
IN THE TRADITIONAL SYSTEM OF THE BAVLI

The ambiguity of the Bavli lies in the unanticipated intersection of a traditional form with a systemic statement. For while set forth in a manner that implicitly bears the attributes of a mere amplification of received truth, as a commentary to the Mishnah, the Bavli viewed in relationship to its sources emerges through a set of purposive choices and therefore is simply not a traditional document. Most of what the Bavli's authorship says simply expresses, in a cogent and coherent way, the topical, rhetorical, and logical choices, forming the well-crafted statement and viewpoint, of its authorship. Little of what the Bavli's authorship presents in a propositional form derives cogency and force from a received statement, and most of it does not. True, many of the propositions address the meaning of paragraphs of the Mishnah, and most of the document is laid out as a commentary to either the Mishnah or Scripture. But the authorship of the Bavli has selected out of Scripture and the Mishnah the passages or topics it wishes to amplify, and therein lies the centerpiece of its autonomous, decision-making attitude toward its own work.

Now, as a matter of fact, the issue of autonomy vs. traditionality defines only beginning the question: no one (outside the circles of the believers) ever imagined that the Bavli's authorship has slavishly taken its message merely from the Mishnah, in which its authorship picks and chooses as much as it does in Scripture. The work of the Bavli's authorship addressed a vast received literature and accomplished the restatement of those parts of the inherited writings that that authorship found pertinent in the presentation of its own system, expressed in a rhetoric of its choice, a logic suitable for its purposes, a topical program deemed relevant to its interests — and all particular to itself and lacking counterpart in other writings. Let me now spell out what the argument of this book requires that we find out concerning the most important writing of a Judaism from the Pentateuchal Judaism to our own day.

Three questions dictate our address to the Bavli. First, is the Bavli an autonomous system or has its authorship produced merely a dependent commentary? Second, does the Bavli utilize logic(s) congruent to its systemic program and purpose (if any)? Third, is the Bavli systemic or traditional, and how does the authorship of the Bavli represent its document in relationship to received writings, e.g., as tradition or free-standing?

The answers to these three questions, which really form one orderly inquiry, will tell us whatever we are going to find out about the structure of the Bavli's authorship's intellect. The proposition is simple: first, the Bavli makes a coherent statement, second, forms a systemic document in traditional form, and, third, utilizes a mixture of logics remarkably suitable to the task of doing just that. The argumentation for these propositions amply serves the task. In demonstrating the autonomy of the Bavli's statement, I set the stage for the argument that the Bavli's statement comes to us within the logic of cogent discourse imparted by argumentation for a theorem and other modes of propositional cogency.

In making manifest the mixed character of the logics of cogent discourse of the Bavli, I show how the Bavli's authorship imparted to their system and its statement in the form of a secondary amplification of an established and given, incrementally expanding truth. In this way we see how that remarkable authorship solved the problem of making a systematic statement of a closed system, yet imputing to the system the standing of a sedimentary and conglomerate tradition of received truth. The attention we have paid to the logics of the Pentateuchal, Essene, and Mishnaic Judaisms required that we correlate systemic intent to logical interiority. Here the correlation forms the crucial step in our inquiry into the structure of intellect that sustains the remarkable document before us. And it will follow, the traditional form of the document constitutes its authorship's solution to the problem, prior to their time never adequately worked out, of how, in a succession to Sinai, to set forth original and well-crafted answers to urgent questions other than those dealt with by the Pentateuchal Judaism (or any of its successors, in sequence). Accordingly, the Bavli's mixture of logics turns out to serve its systemic purposes so well that the Bavli emerges in the form of a tradition while in fact presenting a highly cogent systemic statement.

To revert to the initial stage in our inquiry, we must now ask, precisely in what sense does the Bavli form both a systemic statement and also a traditional document? It is systemic in the presentation of a closed system, a whole, proportioned, and well-composed statement, one that in vast detail blatantly and repetitiously delivered the same self-evidently true answer to the same ponderous and urgent question. But it is traditional in the very real sense that its authorship constantly quotes and cites received writings, laying out its ideas in the form of commentaries to two of those writings, Scripture and the Mishnah, represented as the Torah in two media, written and the oral, respectively. The particular way in which the authorship of the Bavli accomplished this feat is through a fresh conception of the logic of cogent discourse. Specifically, it utilized [1] philosophical logic for the formation of propositions, that is to say, for the drawing of conclusions. But it also made ample and prevailing use of [2] the logic of fixed association for the linking of one proposition to another. In its syllogistic discourse the authorship presented the propositions that, all together, comprised its statement. In organizing that discourse within the discipline of the logic of fixed association, the authorship imparted to its statement the status of tradition, pretending that whatever it had to say constitute a mere clarification of the received Torah, whether oral, in the Mishnah, or written, in Scripture.

Because the Bavli's authorship has imputed to the Mishnah those meanings that that authorship, on the foundations of its own critical judgment and formidable power of logical reasoning in a dialectical movement, itself chose to impute, the Bavli on the face of it presents a system, not merely an incremental tradition. True that reading of the Mishnah became the substance and center of tradition, that is, the ultimate statement, out of late antiquity, of the Judaism of the Dual Torah. But the Bavli's authorship's cogent, rigorously rational reading of the received heritage has demonstrably emerged out of the fresh and sustained, rigorous reflection of its own extended authorship. It did not grow in an organic way in a long process of formulation and transmission of received traditions, in each generation lovingly tended, refined and polished, and handed on essentially as received. The breaks are too sharp, the initiatives too striking, for us to imagine that it did. Not only so, but at any point of entry into the Bavli, opening a page at random, we find ourselves directed by a purposive and well-composed program of inquiry. The authorship, standing at the outset of discourse, knows precisely what it wishes to find out in any passage; it follows a clear-cut program, imposed throughout, a program to be discerned in devices of fixed rhetoric, persistent logical argument, and coherent analytical program, extending over the whole surface of the topical agenda that the authorship has selected.

None of these traits of a coherent and cogent inquiry, so elegantly put together in a single repetitious statement, can be located, in their present combination and structure, in any prior writing. And it did not even form a continuation of the exegetical tradition of the Mishnah formulated by the authorship of the Yerushalmi two hundred years earlier. The breaks from the Mishnah, moreover, are not only in rhetoric and logic and topic. They are marked by a fresh systemic perspective, one that is quite different from that of the Mishnah's and as pervasive, for the Bavli, as the Mishnah's fundamental systemic statement is pervasive in the entirety of the Mishnah. For the Mishnah's authorship set forth a system of sanctification focused on the holiness of the priesthood, the cultic festivals, the Temple and its sacrifices, as well as on the rules for protecting that holiness from Levitical uncleanness — four of the six divisions of the Mishnah on a single theme. The Mishnah's system stresses the issue of sanctification, pure and simple. The Bavli's authorship worked out a system intersecting with the Mishnah's but essentially asymmetrical with it, a system for salvation, focused on the salvific power of the sanctification of the holy people.

A break between the Mishnah's and the Bavli's systems shows us that the Bavli's authorship has made up its own mind and then imputed to a received documents the consequence of its own independent thought. And, as we shall see, the Bavli's authorship accomplished its own goals in its own way, making a statement independent of that of the Mishnah, to which, in form, the Bavli's authorship attached its statement. How then are we to demonstrate the autonomous and fresh character of so protean a statement as the Bavli, showing that that system is not continuous with the one of the Mishnah, but only connected to it? A simple experiment will amply prove the point. For the sake of argument stipulating for the moment that the Bavli's authorship has indeed made a systemic statement, let us ask ourselves whether, on the basis of the system of the Mishnah, we can have predicted through extrapolation from the Mishnah's shape and structure the important components of the statement of the Bavli. The answer is partly affirmative, partly negative — and therefore negative.

The affirmative side is simple to delineate. With only the Mishnah in hand, we can surely outline the main principles of the normative rules that the Bavli incorporates into, and utilizes as the medium for, its systemic statement. But if we knew only the Mishnah's program, we would vastly overstate the range and coverage of the Bavli's, which omits all reference to the Mishnah's first and sixth divisions (Agriculture, save only Blessings, and Purities, except for the rules of Menstrual Uncleanness). And that only suggests the vast disproportions between the Mishnah's authorship's estimates of the attention to be paid to a given range of law, and the decision of the Bavli's authorship on those same matters. The enormous volume of the Bavli's discussion of the three tractates of the Civil Law (Baba Qamma, Baba Mesia, Baba Batra), is out of all proportion to the place that those same tractates occupy within the composition and proportion of the Mishnah. The disproportions form only one indicator of the autonomous judgment exercised by the Bavli's authorship. For once they have chosen their own program of subjects and determined the attention they wish to devote to those subjects, they give evidence of a set of priorities and concerns that are their own and not inherited. Theirs is a fixed and methodical analytical inquiry, which wants to know the same thing about all things.

So I claim that these formal differences point toward substantive systemic choices as well, but among the range of candidates, one demands immediate attention, the systemic teleology, the Mishnah's and the Bavli's. For if I can show a stunning shift in teleological component of a systemic statement, I can fairly claim that the system thereby characterized stands wholly apart from any other (prior) system that sets forth another and different teleology for itself. On that account, we focus, for the systemic cogency of the Bavli as distinct from the writing on which it is supposed to depend for structure and proportion, on that one matter. The teleology of a system answers the question of purpose and goal. It explains why someone should do what the system requires. It may also spell out what will happen if someone does or does not do what the system demands. The Mishnah and its successor-documents, Abot, the Tosefta, in particular, present one picture of the purpose of the system as a whole, a teleology without eschatological focus. The two Talmuds, along with some intermediate documents, later laid forth a different picture, specifically, an eschatological teleology. The documents do cohere. The Talmuds and associated writings of Scripture-exegesis called Midrash, beginning with the former of the two and culminating in the latter, carried forward not only the exegesis of the Mishnah but also the basic values of the Mishnah's system. But they did present substantial changes too, and that is the main point for our purpose.

In concrete terms the indicators are readily at hand. We may not claim that the Mishnah as a document neglects the issue of teleology all together, for the purpose of the document, implicit throughout, is the sanctification of Israel. But that teleology is expressed not through an eschatological myth, such as we are led by Scripture to expect. And that is why, as a matter of fact, that teleology in the Mishnaic system is not so expressed as to form a dominant statement of purpose and goal. Not only so, but the Mishnah's teleology omits reference to history and the end of time, the coming of the Messiah and the last judgment. The Bavli's (in sequence after the Yerushalmi's) focuses upon an eschatological teleology, specifically, the meaning and end of history and the coming of the Messiah. Stated simply, the difference is between a system aiming at the sanctification of Israel in nature in the model of supernature and the sanctification of Israel in the here and the now with the purpose of securing the salvation of Israel at the end of time. To state matters simply, the Mishnah's is a system of sanctification, the Bavli's, one of sanctification for the purpose of salvation. And that restatement of the Mishnah's system accomplishes also the complete reconstitution and revisioning of the received system, drawing the Mishnah's philosophical statement of atemporal and eternal norms into the agenda of changing history and a theology that addresses not rules but one-time events. Clearly, therefore, the two system's — the Mishnah's, the Bavli's — in the critical, I think indicative, matter of teleology, are connected but not continuous. That fact amply justifies the claim that the two form distinct systems. So let us dwell on it.

Among numerous evidences of a shift in teleological thinking from one system to the other, the neglect of the Messiah-theme in the earlier statement and the use of the Messiah-theme in the later document provides the obvious testimony to change, hence to the formation of a new system in part made up autonomously, in part composed of the materials of the old. The philosophers of the Mishnah did not make use of the Messiah myth in the construction of a teleology for their system. They found it possible to present a statement of goals for their projected life of Israel which was entirely separate from appeals to history and eschatology. Since they certainly knew, and even alluded to, long-standing and widely held convictions on eschatological subjects, beginning with those in Scripture, the framers thereby testified that, knowing the larger repertoire, they made choices different from others before and after them. Their document accurately and ubiquitously expresses these choices, both affirmative and negative. The theologians of the Bavli did otherwise. The appearance in the Bavli of a messianic eschatology fully consonant with the larger characteristic of the Rabbinic system — with its stress on the viewpoints and prooftexts of Scripture, its interest in what was happening to Israel, its focus upon the national-historical dimension of the life of the group — indicates that the encompassing Rabbinic system stands essentially autonomous of the prior, Mishnaic system. True, what had gone before was absorbed and fully assimilated. But the Bavli's system, expressed in part in each of the non-Mishnaic segments of the canon, and fully spelled out in all of them, is different in the aggregate from the Mishnaic system.

To state matters in both negative and also positive terms, the Mishnah and its closely related documents, Abot and the Tosefta, do not appeal to the end of time or to eschatology in their framing of their theory of teleology. They speak more commonly about preparing in this world for life in the world to come, and the focus is on the individual and his or her personal salvation, rather than on the nation and its destiny at the end of time. So the Mishnah presented an ahistorical teleology, and did not make use of the messiah-theme to express its teleology. By contrast, the Bavli provides an eschatological and therefore a messiah-centered teleology for its system. That system presents the more familiar teleology of Judaism, which, from the Bavli onward, commonly explains the end and meaning of the system by referring to the end of time and the coming of the Messiah. The teleology takes an eschatological shape, in its appeal to the end of history. Once people speak of the end of time — the eschaton — moreover, they commonly invoke the figure of a messiah, or The Messiah, who will bring on the end and preside over what happens then. The Judaism that emerged from late antiquity therefore took shape as a profoundly eschatological and messianic statement.

The Mishnah's authorship constructed a system in which the entire teleological dimension reached full exposure while hardly invoking the person or functions of a messianic figure of any kind. The Mishnah's non-eschatological teleology would then present a striking contrast to that of the Bavli, which framed the teleological doctrine around the person of the Messiah. The issue of eschatology, framed in mythic terms, further draws in its wake the issue of how history comes to full conceptual expression: the symbolization of things that happen into events, the interpretation of the symbol as history, that is, theology. The Mishnah's framers presented no elaborate theory of events, a fact fully consonant with their systematic points of insistence and encompassing concern. One by one events do not matter. The philosopher-lawyers who made the Mishnah's system as a matter of fact exhibited no theory of history either. Their conception of Israel's destiny in no way called upon historical categories of either narrative or didactic explanation to describe and account for the future. The small importance attributed to the figure of the Messiah as a historical-eschatological figure, therefore, fully accords with the larger traits of the system as a whole. If, as in the Mishnah, what is important in Israel's existence was sanctification, an ongoing process, and not salvation, understood as a one-time event at the end, then no one would find reason to narrate history. Few then would form the obsession about the Messiah so characteristic of Judaism in its later, Rabbinic mode.

Since the Mishnah does speak of a goal and end, we ask, where, if not in the eschaton, or the end of time, do things end? The answer of the Mishnah's system is provided by that system's first and most authoritative apologetic, Abot. There we find that death is the destination. In life we prepare for the voyage. Israel must keep the law in order to make the move required of us all. What is supposed in Abot to make the system work, explaining why we should do the things the Mishnah says, is that other end. It is the end to which history and national destiny prove remote, or, rather, irrelevant. Abot constructs a teleology beyond time, providing a purposeful goal for every individual. Life is the antechamber, death the destination; what we do is weighed and measured. When we die, we stand on one side of the balance, while our life and deeds stand on the other. When we come to the Yerushalmi and the Bavli afterward, the situation changes radically. The figure of the Messiah looms large in both documents. The teleology of the system portrayed in them rests upon the premise of the coming of the Messiah. If one does so and so, the Messiah will come, and if not, the Messiah will tarry. So the compilers and authors of the two Talmuds laid enormous emphasis upon the sin of Israel and the capacity of Israel through repentance both to overcome sin and to bring the Messiah. "The attribute of justice" delays the Messiah's coming. The Messiah will come this very day, if Israel deserves. The Messiah will come when there are no more arrogant ("conceited") Israelites, when judges and officers disappear, when the haughty and judges cease to exist, "Today, if you will obey" (Ps. 95:7).

What alternatives are excluded? First, no one maintains the Messiah will come when the Israelites successfully rebel against Iran or Rome. Second, few express eagerness to live through the coming of the Messiah, the time of troubles marking the event, with the catastrophes, both social and national, that lie in wait. The contrast between this age and the messianic age, moreover, is drawn in some measure in narrowly political terms. Servitude to foreign powers will come to an end. That view proves entirely consistent with opinion, familiar from some of the exegetical collections, that Israel must accept the government of the pagans and that the pagans must not "excessively" oppress Israel. In the hands of the framers of the late canonical literature of Judaism, and in the system of the Bavli in particular, the Messiah serves to keep things pretty much as they are, while at the same time promising dramatic change. The condition of that dramatic change is not richly instantiated. It is given in the most general terms. But it is not difficult to define. Israel must keep God's will, expressed in the Torah and the observance of the rites described therein. So Israel will demonstrate its acceptance of God's rule. While it was first in the Yerushalmi that Judaism drew into its sphere that weighty conception embodied in the Messiah myth, it was in the Bavli that the matter came to its fullest expression.

Before turning to the logic of cogent discourse that characterizes the statement, therefore the writing, of the Bavli's authorship, let me generalize from this stunning initiative on the part of the Bavli's authorship to a more encompassing observation on the systemic traits of their statement as a whole. In the Bavli we witness a striking reversion to biblical convictions about the centrality of history in the definition of Israel's reality.

The heavy weight of prophecy, apocalyptic, and biblical historiography, with their emphasis upon salvation and on history as the indicator of Israel's salvation, stood against the Mishnah's quite separate thesis of what truly mattered. What, from the Bavli's sages' viewpoint, demanded description and analysis and required interpretation? It was the category of sanctification, for eternity. The true issue framed by history and apocalypse was how to move toward the foreordained end of salvation, how to act in time to reach salvation at the end of the time. The Mishnah's teleology beyond time and its capacity to posit an eschatology without a place for a historical Messiah take a position beyond that of the entire antecedent sacred literature of Israel. Only one strand, the priestly one, had ever taken so extreme a position on the centrality of sanctification and the peripheral nature of salvation. Wisdom had stood in between, with its own concerns, drawing attention both to what happened and to what endured. But to Wisdom what finally mattered was not nature or supernature, but rather abiding relationships in historical time.

The framers of the Mishnah had found it possible to construct a complete and encompassing teleology for their system with scarcely a single word about the Messiah's coming at that time when the system would be perfectly achieved. We must not lose sight of the importance of the fundamental message, with its emphasis on repentance, on the one side, and the power of Israel to reform itself, on the other. The Messiah will come any day that Israel makes it possible.

Let me underline the most important statement of this large conception: If all Israel will keep a single Sabbath in the proper (Rabbinic) way, the Messiah will come. If all Israel will repent for one day, the Messiah will come. "Whenever you want ...," the Messiah will come. Now, two things are happening here. First, the system of religious observance, including study of Torah, is explicitly invoked as having salvific power. Second, the persistent hope of the people for the coming of the Messiah is linked to the system of Rabbinic observance and belief. In this way, the austere program of the Mishnah develops in a different direction, with no trace of a promise that the Messiah will come if and when the system is fully realized. Here a teleology lacking all eschatological dimension gives way to an explicitly messianic statement that the purpose of the law is to attain Israel's salvation: "If you want it, God wants it too." The one thing Israel commands is its own heart; the power it yet exercises is the power to repent. These suffice. The entire history of humanity will respond to Israel's will, to what happens in Israel's heart and soul. With the Temple in ruins, repentance can take place only within the heart and mind.

Israel may contribute to its own salvation, by the right attitude and the right deed. But Israel bears responsibility for its present condition. So what Israel does makes history. Any account of the Messiah-doctrine of the Bavli must lay appropriate stress on that conviction: Israel makes its own history, therefore shapes its own destiny. This lesson, sages maintained, derives from the very condition of Israel even then, its suffering and its despair. How so? History taught moral lessons. Historical events entered into the construction of a teleology for the Bavli's system of Judaism as a whole. What the law demanded reflected the consequences of wrongful action on the part of Israel. So, again, Israel's own deeds defined the events of history. Rome's role, like Assyria's and Babylonia's, depended upon Israel's provoking divine wrath as it was executed by the great empire. The paradox of the Bavli's system of history and Messiah lies in the fact that Israel can free itself of control by other nations only by humbly agreeing to accept God's rule. The nations — Rome, in the present instance — rest on one side of the balance, while God rests on the other. Israel must then choose between them. There is no such thing for Israel as freedom from both God and the nations, total autonomy and independence. There is only a choice of masters, a ruler on earth or a ruler in heaven. In the Talmud's theory of salvation, therefore, the framers provided Israel with an account of how to overcome the unsatisfactory circumstances of an unredeemed present, so as to accomplish the movement from here to the much-desired future. When the Talmud's authorities present statements on the promise of the law for those who keep it, therefore, they provide glimpses of the goal of the system as a whole. These invoked the primacy of the rabbi and the legitimating power of the Torah, and in those two components of the system we find the principles of the Messianic doctrine. And these bring us back to the argument with Christ triumphant, as the Christians perceived him.

What is most interesting in Bavli's picture is that the hope for the Messiah's coming is further joined to the moral condition of each individual Israelite. Hence the messianic fulfillment was made to depend on the repentance of Israel. The entire drama, envisioned by others in earlier types of Judaism as a world-historical event, was reworked in context into a moment in the life of the individual and the people of Israel collectively. The coming of the Messiah depended not on historical action but on moral regeneration. So from a force that moved Israelites to take up weapons on the battlefield, the messianic hope and yearning were transformed into motives for spiritual regeneration and ethical behavior. The energies released in the messianic fervor were then linked to rabbinical government, through which Israel would form the godly society. When we reflect that the message, "If you want it, He too wants it to be," comes in a generation confronting a dreadful disappointment, its full weight and meaning become clear. Now to the intellectual core, the mind, the inside of the system, the interior structure of cogent discourse that sustains the statement we have briefly surveyed. Let me generalize from the exemplary case of the teleology of the Mishnaic as against the Bavli's systems. The Bavli simply cannot be shown systematically and generally to continue the program and inquiry of predecessors. Therefore with the Bavli a new tradition got underway, and the Bavli does not wholly depend upon, and restate, a prior tradition in the sense just now spelled out. For in few ways does the Bavli give evidence of taking its place within such a process of tradition, and we cannot appeal to the document to demonstrate that the authorship of the Bavli represented itself as traditional and its work as authoritative on that account.

This is not to propose that the Bavli's system is utterly unrelated to that of the Mishnah, any more than the Mishnah's stands autonomous of Scripture. Quite the opposite, the Bavli's framers have made ample use of received ("traditional") materials, both scriptural and Mishnaic, as well as deriving from other past writings. But these they used for their own purposes and in their own ways. In the case at hand, for instance, in both statements, the matter of the Messiah remained subordinated: "If you do this or that, the Messiah will come." The Messiah myth supplied the fixed teleology for the variety of ineluctable demands of the system as a whole. In fact what happened was that the Rabbinic system of the Bavli transformed the Messiah-myth in its totality into an essentially ahistorical force. If people wanted to reach the end of time, they had to rise above time, that is, history, and stand off at the side of great ephemeral movements of political and military character. That is the message of the Messiah-myth as it reaches full exposure in the Rabbinic system of the Bavli. At its foundation it is precisely the message of the teleology without eschatology expressed by the Mishnah and its associated documents. Accordingly, we cannot claim that the Bavli's system in this regard constitutes a reaction against the Mishnaic one. We must conclude, quite to the contrary, that in the Talmuds and their associated documents we see the restatement, in classical-mythic form, of the ontological convictions that had informed the minds of the second-century philosophers of the Mishnah. The new medium, taking the form of a theology of history, contained the old, enduring message: Israel must turn away from time and change, submit to whatever happens, so as to win for itself the only government worth having, that is, God's rule, accomplished through God's anointed agent, the Messiah.

The two systems, the Mishnah's and the Bavli's, therefore

prove connected but not continuous. On that basis I can characterize, as I do, the Bavli's as a system, not merely the amplification or adaptation of a tradition from we know not where. It is a system in its fundamental structure, turning in upon itself, closed, proportioned, well-composed. But at the same time, in form, and in the present case, in position as well, it also is traditional in its relationship to prior systems, as we see so clearly in this indicative case. Accordingly, seen in this way, the Bavli's statement is both traditional and also systemic. That we see in the critical issue of systemic teleology. What about logic? It is the mark of the genius of the Bavli's authorship that it found appropriate logics — not one but two of them — to sustain and direct the entirety of the discourse that it proposed to set forth. The logic matched the treatment of the topic: a system that rewrites a prior and received system, hence, in an odd way, what I call, by way of irony, a traditional system. Let me leave no doubt of the upshot of the matter: a traditional system by definition is systemic, exhibiting all the traits I imputed in Chapter Three to a free-standing system. But we miss the aesthetic and intellectual character of the Bavli, hence of the intellect of Judaism defined by studying the Bavli for endless generations thereafter, if we characterize the Bavli as a system as free-standing as the Mishnah's or the Pentateuch's. Its authorship did not pretend to begin afresh; to the contrary, the writers of the Bavli subordinated their entire statement to the form of tradition. But at the same time, the Bavli's authorship made its own decisions and set forth its own statement, and it did so with that same courageous independence of mind that we uncover, to begin with, in the writers who made up a world and said that God had done it.

    We have now tested the hypothesis that the Bavli forms an essentially traditional document and the further claim that the reason for the Bavli's traditional — and, by the way, canonical — status lies in its success in completing work begun by the predecessors of the document, for instance, the Yerushalmi. True enough, the Bavli contains ample selections from available writings. The authorship of the Bavli leaves no doubt that it makes extensive use of extant materials, sayings and stories. The Bavli's authorship further takes as its task the elucidation of the received code, the Mishnah. More to the point, frequent citations of materials now found in the Tosefta as well as allusions to sayings framed in Tannaite Hebrew and attributed to Tannaite authority — marked, for instance, by TN' — time and again alert us to extensive reference, by our authorship, to a prior corpus of materials. Not only so, but contemporary scholarship has closely read both brief sayings and also extended discourses in light of two or three or more versions and come to the conclusion that a later generation has taken up and made use of available materials. Most strikingly of all, our authorship claims in virtually every line to come at the end of a chain of tradition, since the bulk of the generative sayings — those that form the foundation for sustained inquiry and dialectical discourse — is assigned to named authorities clearly understood to stand prior to the work of the ultimate redactors. Even if we preserve a certain reluctance to take at face value all of these attributions to prior authorities, we have to take full account of the authorship's insistence upon its own traditionality. In all of these ways, the authorship of the Bavli so represents itself as to claim that, assuredly, it stands in a line of tradition, taking over and reworking received materials, restating viewpoints that originate in prior ages. And that fact makes all the more striking the fundamental autonomy of discourse displayed by the document at the end. So let us serve as interlocutors for the great authorship at hand and present some pointed questions.

Were we therefore to enter into conversation with the penultimate and ultimate authorship of the Bavli, the first thing we should want to know is simple: what have you made up? And what have you simply repeated out of a long-continuing heritage of formulation and transmission? And why should we believe you? The authorship then would be hard put to demonstrate in detail that its fundamental work of literary selection and ordering, its basic choices on sustained and logical discourse, its essential statement upon the topics it has selected — that anything important in their document derives from long generations past.

Should they say, "Look at the treatment of the Mishnah," we should answer, "But did you continue the Yerushalmi's program or did you make up your own?" And in the total candor we rightly impute to that remarkable authorship, the Bavli's compositors would say, "It is our own — demonstrably so."

And if we were to say, "To what completed documents have you resorted for a ready-made program?" our soi-disant - traditionalists would direct our attention to the Tosefta, their obvious (and sole) candidate. And, if they were to do so, we should open the Tosefta's treatment of, or counterpart to, a given chapter of the Mishnah and look in vain for a systematic, orderly, and encompassing discourse, dictated by the order and plan of the Tosefta, out of which our authorship has composed a sizable and sustained statement.

And when, finally, we ask our authorship to state its policy in regard to Scripture and inquire whether or not a sustained and ongoing tradition of exegesis of Scripture has framed discourse, the reply will prove quite simple. "We looked for what we wanted to seek, and we found it." Traditionalists indeed!

These four loci at which boundaries may have merged, and intersections turned into commonalities, therefore mark walled and sealed borders. A received heritage of sayings and stories may have joined our authorship to its teachers and their teachers — but not to that larger community of sustained learning that stands behind the entirety of the writings received as authoritative, or even a sizable proportion of those writings. The presence, in the ultimate statement of the Bavli, of sayings imputed to prior figures — back to Scripture, back to Sinai — testifies only to the workings of a canon of taste and judgment to begin with defined and accepted as definitive by those who defined it: the authorship at hand itself. The availability, to our authorship, of a systematic exegesis of the same Mishnah-chapter has not made self-evident to our authorship the work of continuation and completion of a prior approach. Quite to the contrary, we deal with an authorship of amazingly independent mind, working independently and in an essentially original way on materials on which others have handed on a quite persuasive and cogent statement. Tosefta on the one side, Scripture and a heritage of conventional reading thereof on the other — neither has defined the program of our document or determined the terms in which it would make its statement, though both, in a subordinated position and in a paltry limited measure, are given some sort of a say. The Bavli is connected to a variety of prior writings but continuous with none of them.

The upshot is simple. The Bavli in relationship to its sources is not a traditional document, in the plain sense that most of what it says in a cogent and coherent way expresses the well-crafted statement and viewpoint of its authorship in particular. Excluding, of course, the Mishnah, to which the Bavli devotes its sustained and systematic attention, little of what our authorship says derives cogency and force from a received statement. Most does not. But that is only beginning the question: no one (outside the circles of the believers) ever said that the Bavli's authorship has slavishly taken its message merely from the Mishnah, in which its authorship picks and chooses as much as it does in Scripture, first of all deciding to deal with thirty-seven tractates and to ignore twenty-five. The Bavli's authorship's cogent, rigorously rational reading of the received heritage has demonstrably emerged not from a long process of formulation and transmission of received traditions, in each generation lovingly tended, refined and polished, and handed on essentially as received. Indeed, to revert to the opening question of the preface, I should doubt that it could have, for the literary evidence we have examined hardly suggests that a system of applied reason and sustained, rigorously rational inquiry can coexist with a process of tradition.

What then holds the whole together? It is, as we presently shall see in our sample, that logic of fixed association that effects the linkage between completed thoughts, fully spelled out, not in a topical sequence established to argue for yet larger propositions, but in a sequence defined by an external connection, one with no propositional substance whatsoever. Stated simply for the case of the Bavli, we work out our propositions as paragraphs of completed, syllogistic thought and argument. But then we link one to the next by reference to the sentences of the Mishnah, read one by one. So the cogent discourse at the level of drawing conclusions is philosophical, while discourse is held together at the logic of the large-scale making of connection through a fixed associations formally extrinsic to discourse. Laying matters out as a commentary to the Mishnah is the result of this mixture of two logics. Let us then consider once again the traits of the logic of fixed association, which serves our authorship so effectively in imparting the form of tradition to the structure of a systemic system they have composed for us.

The logic of fixed association connects into protracted statements of a cogent character otherwise unrelated sequential sentences, and also joins into sizable compositions entire paragraphs that on their own, through their own propositions, in no way coalesce. Among the documents that reached closure prior to the conclusion of the Bavli, few are wholly put together in such a way that the logic of fixed association prevails both in composing sentences into paragraphs and also in establishing the intelligible connection and order of large units of thought, that is, whole paragraphs, whether propositional or otherwise.

Let us rapidly review the criteria for the logic of fixed association. The negative criteria are, first, that the sentences, two or more, do not all together yield a statement that transcends the sum of the parts. Fixed associative compositions moreover do not gain cogency through statements of propositions. The sentences are cogent, but the cogency derives from a source other than shared propositions or participation in an argument yielding a shared proposition. The fixed association that effects connection for cogent discourse derives, it follows, from a "text" outside of the composition at hand and known to, taken for granted by, the composition at hand.

True, that "text" may be a list of names; it may be a received document or portion thereof. But it is the given, and its cogency is the single prevailing premise that otherwise unrelated facts belong together in some sort of established sequence and order. While some of the sentences joined together in a statement the cogency of which appeals to fixed association may on their own make quite cogent points, and all of them are surely intelligible as discrete statements, the lot of them form a chaotic composite, except that the authorship of the document assigns them to the rubric defined by the named authority.

The logic of fixed association shows radical limitations characteristic of a mode of thought that joins A to 3 because both A and 3 refer back to a common point, represented here by the symbol #. That mode of thought is fundamentally alien to the orderly pursuit of logical inquiry familiar in the Western philosophical and scientific tradition, because, carried to its logical conclusion, that logic never requires its practitioner to make connections; these are invariably supplied, imputed, never discovered, never source of stimulus to curiosity.

This brings us to the demonstration of how the authorship of the Bavli have composed their document, in the making of medium- and large-scale logical connections, by resort to two distinct principles of cogent discourse. These are, first, the one of propositional connection within completed units of thought, a connection discovered through the pursuit of reasoned speculative inquiry, and second, the other of the fixed associative connection between and among those same completed units of thought, producing large-scale compositions. Sizable numbers of the completed units of thought of the Bavli find inner cogency through the development of a proposition concerning a given theme. Overall, these units of completed thought are linked to one another through the connections supplied for the Bavli extrinsically by both the Mishnah and Scripture. The framers of the Bavli had in hand a tripartite corpus of inherited materials awaiting composition into a final, closed document. First, they took up materials, in various states and stages of completion, pertinent to the Mishnah or to the principles of laws that the Mishnah had originally brought to articulation. Second, they had in hand received materials, again in various conditions, pertinent to the Scripture, both as the Scripture related to the Mishnah and also as the Scripture laid forth its own narratives. And that fact points to the way in which the logic of fixed association governed their work.

Let me now give an example of the way in which I conceive the Bavli's framers to have made use of the logic of fixed association in that dual way that involved appeal for cogency to both the Mishnah and Scripture. Once more I turn to a familiar item, namely, Mishnah-tractate Sanhedrin Chapter Two, now as the Bavli's authorship presents the matter. Since our interest is in identifying passages in which both the Mishnah and Scripture serve to hold together discrete compositions, ordinarily of a propositional character, I give only highlights. These will then illustrate the workings of the logic of fixed association in the Bavli. The numbers in square brackets refer to the Bavli's pagination.

Bavli-tractate Sanhedrin to Mishnah-tractate Sanhedrin
2:3
- A. [If] [the king] suffers a death in his family, he does not leave the gate of his palace.
- B. R. Judah says, "If he wants to go out after the bier, he goes out,
- C. "for thus we find in the case of David, that he went out after the bier of Abner,
- D. "since it is said, 'And King David followed the bier' (2 Sam. 3:31)."
- E. They said to him, "This action was only to appease the people."
- F. And when they provide him with the funeral meal, all the people sit on the ground, while he sits on a couch.

I
- A. Our rabbis have taught on Tannaite authority:
- B. In a place in which women are accustomed to go forth after the bier, they go forth in that way. If they are accustomed to go forth before the bier, they go forth in that manner.
- C. R. Judah says, "Women always go forth in front of the bier.
- D. "For so we find in the case of David that he went forth after the bier of Abner.
- E. "For it is said, 'And King David followed the bier' (2 Sam. 3:31)."
- F. They said to him, "That was only to appease the people [M. 2:3D-E].
- G. "They were appeased, for David would go forth among the men and come in among the women, go forth among the women and come in among the men,
- H. "as it is said, 'So all the people and all Israel understood that it was not of the king to slay Abner' (2 Sam. 3:37)."

The Bavli's authorship now inserts a sizable exposition on David's relationship with Abner, and this goes its own way, without regard to the amplification of M. Sanhedrin 2:3D-E, cited just now. The following not-very-cogent unit of discourse makes no single point but holds together because of the systematic amplification of the cited verses. No. II stands by itself and sets the stage for what is to follow.

II

A. Raba expounded, "What is the meaning of that which is written, 'And all the people came to cause David to eat bread' (2 Sam. 3:35)?

B. "It was written, 'to pierce David' [with a K], but we read, 'to cause him to eat bread' [with a B].

C. "To begin with they came to pierce him but in the end to cause him to eat bread."

III

A. Said R. Judah said Rab, "On what account was Abner punished? Because he could have prevented Saul but did not prevent him [from killing the priest of Nob, 1 Sam. 22:18]."

B. R. Isaac said, "He did try to prevent him, but he got no response."

C. And both of them interpret the same verse of Scripture: "And the king lamented for Abner and said, Should Abner die as a churl dies, your hands were not bound or your feet put into fetters" (2 Sam. 2:33).

D. He who maintains that he did not try to stop Saul interprets the verse in this way: "Your hands were not bound nor were your feet put into fetters" — so why did you not try to stop him? "As a man falls before the children of iniquity so did you fall" (2 Sam. 3:33).

E. He who maintains that he did try to stop Saul but got no response interprets the verse as an expression of amazement: "Should he have died as a churl dies? Your hands were not bound and your feet were not put into fetters."

F. Since he did protest, why "As a man falls before the children of iniquity, so did you fall"?

G. In the view of him who has said that he did protest, why was he punished?

H. Said R. Nahman bar Isaac, "Because he held up the coming of the house of David by two and a half years."

The framer reverts to the Mishnah-passage and proceeds. What we have now is the familiar program of Mishnah-exegesis: amplification of words and phrases in the instance of No. IV, of which I present only a few stichs.

IV

    A. And when they provide him with the funeral meal, [all the people sit on the ground, while he sits on a couch] [M. 2:3F]:

    B. What is the couch?

    C. Said Ulla, "It is a small couch."

    D. Said rabbis to Ulla, "Now is there something on which, up to that time, he had never sat, and now we seat him on that object?"

    E. Raba objected to this argument, "What sort of problem is this? Perhaps it may be compared to the matter of eating and drinking, for up to this point we gave him nothing to eat or drink, while now we bring him food and drink...."

The ongoing discussion of the matter provides a secondary development of the rules pertaining to the couch under discussion and need not detain us. Yet another example of a sizable composition appealing for cogency to Scripture is tacked on to M. 2:4A-D. Here is another composition that holds together solely because of reference to verses of Scripture. Specifically, 2 Sam. 13 forms the center, and the various sentences then are joined to that center, but not to one another:

III

    A. Said R. Judah said Rab, "David had four hundred sons, all of them born of beautiful captive women. All grew long locks plaited down the back. All of them seated in golden chariots.

    B. "And they went forth at the head of troops, and they were the powerful figures in the house of David."

    C. And R. Judah said Rab said, "Tamar was the daughter of a beautiful captive woman.

    D. "For it is said, 'Now, therefore, I pray you, speak to the king, for he will not withhold me from you' (2 Sam. 13:13).

E. "Now if you hold that she was the daughter of a valid marriage, would the king ever have permitted [Amnon] to marry his sister?"

F. "But, it follows, she was the daughter of a beautiful captive woman."

G. "And Amnon had a friend, whose name was Jonadab, son of Shimeah, David's brother, and Jonadab was a very subtle man" (2 Sam. 13:3): Said R. Judah said Rab, "He was subtle about doing evil."

H. "And he said to him, Why, son of the king, are you thus becoming leaner... And Jonadab said to him, Lay down on your bed and pretend to be sick... and she will prepare the food in my sight... and she took the pan and poured [the cakes] out before him" (2 Sam. 13:4ff.): Said R. Judah said Rab, "They were some sort of pancakes."

I. "Then Amnon hated her with a very great hatred" (2 Sam. 13:15): What was the reason?

J. Said R. Isaac, "One of his hairs got caught [around his penis and cut it off] making him one whose penis had been cut off."

K. But was she the one who had tied the hair around his penis? What had she done?

L. Rather, I should say, she had tied a hair around his penis and made him into one whose penis had been cut off.

M. Is this true? And did not Raba explain, "What is the sense of the verse, 'And your renown went forth among the nations for your beauty' (Ez. 16:14)? It is that Israelite women do not have armpit or pubic hair."

N. Tamar was different, because she was the daughter of a beautiful captive woman.

O. "And Tamar put ashes on her head and tore her garment of many colors" (2 Sam. 13:19):

P. It was taught on Tannaite authority in the name of R. Joshua b. Qorhah, "Tamar established a high wall at that time [protecting chastity]. People said, 'If such could happen to princesses, all the more so can it happen to ordinary women.' If such could happen to virtuous women, all the more so can it happen to wanton ones!"

Q. Said R. Judah said Rab, "At that time they made a decree [21B] against a man's being alone with any woman

[married or] unmarried."
R. But the rule against a man's being alone with [a married woman] derives from the authority of the Torah [and not from the authority of rabbis later on].
S. For R. Yohanan said in the name of R. Simeon b. Yehosedeq, "Whence in the Torah do we find an indication against a man's being alone [with a married woman]? As it is said, 'If your brother, son of your mother, entice you' (Deut. 13:7).
T. "And is it the fact that the son of one's mother can entice, but the son of the father cannot entice? Rather, it is to tell you that a son may be alone with his mother, and no one else may be alone with any of the consanguineous female relations listed in the Torah."
U. Rather, they made a decree against a man's being alone with an unmarried woman.
V. "And Adonijah, son of Haggith, exalts himself, saying, I will be king" (1 Kgs. 1:5):
W. Said R. Judah said Rab, "This teaches that he tried to fit [the crown on his head], but it would not fit."
X. "And he prepares chariots and horses and fifty men to run before him" (1 Kgs. 1:5):
Y. So what was new [about princes' having retinues]?
Z. Said R. Judah said Rab, "All of them had had their spleen removed [believed to make them faster runners] and the flesh of the soles of their feet cut off [Shachter, p. 115, n. 12: so that they might be fleet of foot and impervious to briars and thorns]."

My final example of how Scripture serves to connect one sentence to another shows us, from the citation of the Mishnah onward, a systematic interest not in the Mishnah but in Scripture and its exposition.

Bavli-tractate Sanhedrin to Mishnah-tractate Sanhedrin 2:5
A. **[Others may] not ride on his horse, sit on his throne, handle his scepter.**
B. And [others may] not watch him while he is getting a haircut, or while he is nude, or in the bath-house,

I

    C. since it is said, "You shall surely set him as king over you" (Deut. 17:15) — that reverence for him will be upon you.

I

    A. Said R. Jacob said R. Yohanan, "Abishai would have been permitted to be married to Solomon, but was forbidden to be married to Adonijah.

    B. "She would have been permitted to Solomon, because he was king, and the king is permitted to make use of the scepter of [a former] king.

    C. "But she was forbidden to Adonijah, for he was an ordinary person."

II

    A. And what is the story of Abishai?

    B. It is written, "King David was old, stricken in years.... His servants said to him, Let there be sought..." And it is written, "They sought for him a pretty girl..." and it is written, "And the girl was very fair, and she became a companion to the king and ministered to him" (1 Kgs. 1:1-5).

    C. She said to him, "Let's get married."

    D. He said to her, "You are forbidden to me."

    E. She said to him, "When the thief fears for his life, he seizes virtue."

    F. He said to them, "Call Bath Sheba to me."

    G. And it is written, "And Bath Sheba went into the king to the chamber" (1 Kgs. 1:15).

    H. Said R. Judah said Rab, "At that time [having had sexual relations with David] Bath Sheba wiped herself with thirteen cloths [to show that he was hardly impotent, contrary to Abishag's accusation]."

    I. Said R. Shemen bar Abba, "Come and take note of how difficult is an act of divorce.

    J. "For lo, they permitted King David to be alone [with the woman], but they did not permit him to divorce [one of his other wives]...."

The exposition of the Mishnah hardly requires insertion of these materials, the cogency of which derives rather from Scripture. Now let me return to the argument overall and state matters in general terms. A further repertoire of examples of the operation of the logic of fixed association, in the Bavli's case defined by both the

Mishnah and Scripture, its themes or its sequential verses, is not required to make the simple point at hand. Let me now generalize on the example before us.

Two principal sources of fixed associations served the Bavli's framers, the Mishnah and Scripture. The authorships of the tractates of the Bavli in general first of all organized the Bavli around the Mishnah, just as the framers of the Yerushalmi had done. Second, they adapted and included vast tracts of antecedent materials organized as scriptural commentary. These they inserted whole and complete, not at all in response to the Mishnah's program. They never created redactional compositions of a sizable order that focused upon given authorities, even though sufficient materials lay at hand to allow doing so. They joined the Mishnah to Scripture in such a way as to give final form and fixed expression, through their categories of the organization of all knowledge, to the Torah as it had been known, sifted, searched, approved, and handed down, even from the remote past to their own day. Accordingly, the Bavli's ultimate framers made the decision to present large-scale discussions along lines of order and sequence dictated not by topics and propositional arguments concerning them — as had Aphrahat, for instance, in his demonstrations. Rather they selected the two components of the one whole Torah, oral and written, of Moses, our rabbi, at Sinai, and these they set forth as the connections that held together and ordered all discourse. That is how they organized what they knew, on the one side, and made their choices in laying out the main lines of the structure of knowledge, on the other.

Let me now generalize on the traits of the simple example just now reviewed. The Bavli is made up of sizable systematic statements of propositions, syllogistic arguments fully worked out and elegantly exposed. Accordingly, two principles of logical discourse are at play. For the statement of propositions, sizable arguments and proofs, the usual philosophical logic dictates the joining of sentence to sentences and the composition of paragraphs, that is, completed thoughts. For the presentation of the whole, the other logic, the one deriving from imputed, fixed associations, external to the propositions at hand, serves equally well. The framers of the Bavli drew together the results of work which people prior to their own labors already had completed. Available as both completed documents and also sizable components, statements awaiting agglutination or conglomeration in finished documents, these ready-made materials were sewn together with only one kind of thread. Whatever the place and role of the diverse types of logics that formed the compositions circulating before and in the time of the Bavli — compilations of scriptural exegeses, the Yerushalmi, not to mention the exegeses of Pentateuchal laws in Sifra and the two Sifrés, the Tosefta, The Fathers [Avot] and The Fathers According to Rabbi Nathan, Genesis Rabbah, Leviticus Rabbah, Pesiqta deRab Kahana, and on and on — the Bavli superseded them all and defined the mind of Judaism. It was through the Bavli that the entire antecedent canon reached the Judaism of the Dual Torah beyond the formative age.

At the outset I asked three questions, concerning whether or not the Bavli makes a systemic statement on its own, the definition of the logics of cogent discourse used by the framers, and the classification of the Bavli's authorship's statement (if it was a statement) as systemic or traditional. We now recognize that the authorship of the Bavli by the criterion of its teleological position assuredly made an autonomous statement of its own, one that, moreover, constitutes the statement of a system. That statement bore the marks of connection to, but not continuity with, the system of the Mishnah. While the systemic statement bore its own distinctive message, however, it came forth in the form of a traditional and (merely) incremental account of how things had happened to attach themselves to received truth. And this leads us to the final point of our inquiry: how does the authorship of the Bavli situate its statement in relationship to the received heritage identified by them as authoritative, meaning, in this context, to the Pentateuchal Judaism? System-builders prior to the Bavli had taken a position of benign neglect of their predecessors, if they acknowledged any. The Pentateuchal case of course is extreme: reworking a vast corpus of received writing, the authorship acknowledged no past but Sinai. But the Mishnah's, in context, is no less striking in its indifference to, e.g., supplying proof-texts from Scripture for all of its statements or even more than a negligible minority of them.

On the surface, then, the Bavli's authorship broke new ground among system-builders by adopting the form of a commentary to the Mishnah and Scripture for its systemic statement. Implicitly, after all, the message was clear. The commentary-form bore the message that the Bavli's authorship stood in a line of continuing tradition, even while that authorship presented a systemic statement of its own shaping. How to accomplish, in form, precisely what, in mind and intellect, the authorship before us had in mind? The logic of fixed association is what permitted the Bavli's authorships to appeal to two distinct repertoires of sequential items, the Mishnah and also Scripture. The use of the logic of fixed association served a critical theological purpose, specifically, facilitating the linkage into a single statement ("the one whole Torah") of the two Torahs, oral and written, that is, the Mishnah and Scripture. That is the effect of the Bavli's layout as a commentary to the Mishnah or to Scripture.

As between the two kinds of logic relevant in this context — propositional and fixed associative — the Bavli appealed for ultimate composition, for the deep structure and cogency of all learning, therefore all thought worth thinking, to the latter. The Bavli defined the mind of Judaism and imparted to Judaic thought, inculcated in enduring institutions of learning but also in implicit patterns of public discourse, the logics that would predominate, both propositional and otherwise. The Bavli made all the difference, because made room for propositional discourse at that middle range of knowledge that made of the parts autonomous statements of one thing or another, then also put all knowledge together in its own rather odd way, by the imputed and extrinsic associations dictated by Scripture and the Mishnah. Judaic thought therefore yielded not a series of treatises on topics and propositions, but a series of medium-length discourses that gain cogency imposed only from without. The upshot for the Bavli's authorship was to yield a systemic statement in the form of a traditional document.

What happened then? The Bavli imposed its model upon the

intellect of Judaism for the next millennium and beyond. For the impact of this mixed logic of cogency upon the intellect of Judaism was to stimulate one kind of thinking and not another. Propositional thought of a philosophical character could go forward. But in form, and therefore, in interior structure, propositional thinking standing on its own in the centers of Torah-study defined by the mind of the Bavli, would not yield that kind of abstract speculation, independent of all connections except those implicit in propositions, characteristic of philosophy, including natural philosophy. Skepticism would flourish, contention and criticism would abound. An intellectual world defined in this way found ample stimulus for speculation, but not for that kind of speculation that, to begin with, without a public agenda and without an a priori system would address the issue of connection between one thing and something else. For the Mishnah or Scripture, or even the lives and teachings of holy men, imparted to two or more discrete facts that connection that led to the drawing of conclusions and the framing of theses for inquiry, at least so far as the Bavli's treatises' authorships exemplified the logic defining the mind of Judaism.

One final question awaits: how does the Bavli's authorship's work compare to that of the Pentateuch's? So now let us turn matters around and conduct a final mental experiment. If we make up a conversation between the Bavli's authorship and the framers of the Pentateuch, what sort of exchange can we imagine? Specifically, were the Jewish framers of the Pentateuch to confront the work of the authorship of the Bavli, would they have recognized a mind of Judaism similar to their own? Properly introduced to what is at stake here, they would, I maintain, have said yes. What would have struck them as affirmative arguments? In the Bavli's anonymity, in its sustained discourse in behalf of "the community" or the consensus of sages, in its encompassing consistency and engaging mode of insistence on a single point in many particulars, yes, I think the Pentateuchal authorship will have found their own traits of mind and discourse in the Bavli's framers' work. But I wonder whether they should also have accorded complete respect to an authorship that, so unlike themselves, claimed for its ideas second place, in a sequence of tradition tacking them on to a prior and received document.

After all, the great intellects of the Pentateuch will have wondered, why not do what their near-contemporaries had done in rewriting J, E, JE, P, and D, to produce the Pentateuch (not to mention the nearly-contemporary work of paraphrasing the books of Samuel and Kings in such a way as to produce the books of Chronicles)? For they had simply taken received materials and recast them in terms, and also in language, of their own. Why not, then, just rewrite the Mishnah, inserting, to take to be the case I introduced at the outset, the conception of an eschatological teleology represented by a Messiah in places where the theme does not appear? Or, lacking the boldness of the Chronicler(s) (not to mention the Pentateuchal compilers and revisers themselves!), the framers of the Bavli can at least allude to received materials without explicitly citing them in a way that preserved their distinct standing as an autonomous document? Many writers, both prior to, and in the time of, the Pentateuchal ones did just that, making reference to established facts of life and thought without citing, in a slavish, academic way, the documents that preserved those facts. The authorships of the Pentateuch and of the Mishnah set forth systems in utter indifference to the category, tradition. And, I think it is clear, to the degree that the Essene library at Qumran represents a system, the writers there also made the same choice.

Why then did the Bavli's framers present as traditional what was, in fact, an independent and autonomous reshaping of inherited materials within a mold they themselves had made up? The answer to that question carries us into a set of issues that find resolution far beyond the sources on which we concentrate here. The form of commentary by itself is not pertinent to the answer, since, as we noted earlier, it is the logic, not the form, that imparts cultural significance to modes of cogent discourse. But we can point to a problem that the Bavli's authorship successfully solved. How was a later generation to work out its received legacy of revealed truth without collapsing under the weight of tradition? The Bavli's framers found the way in which a set of philosophers, forming a system with its own generative principles of order, proportion, composition, and of course mode of logic to carry on cogent discourse, might relate its philosophical work to its larger historical context. And in solving that problem as they did, the Bavli's system-builders discovered in the detail of their document the way for holding together in a fructifying tension continuity and change, permanence and spontaneity, charisma and routine (in terms our generation itself has received from its masters), culture and creativity, and, reaching outward beyond the limits of culture, nature and nurture.

For philosophy and system-building did not, and do not, take place fresh, even though, in logic and order, they are possible only when formed of the elaboration of first principles. On the contrary, thought forms a component of on-going society, and systems restate received facts of everyday reality. Thought, after all, does not begin with thinking about thought, though it may end there. The Bavli then presents us with the answer that would characterize the mind of Judaism from then to now to the question of how to hold together in fruitful tension tradition and system, history and philosophy, the continuity and change that unite past, present, and future. But that was not the only answer of the classical age, as we see when we compare the Bavli to the Bible. For the invention of the Bible points toward antiquity's other important way of sorting out and holding together sustaining tradition and new thought. Receiving diverse systems of thought or fragments thereof, the intellect behind the Bible represented these diverse and contradictory writings as a single cogent system, essentially doing the opposite of what the Bavli's authorship did, while producing the same result: a traditional system. And for the intellects formed in the Bavli and in the Bible alike, that is how, for the history of the West, civilization would endure, with roots, but also growth and change. For, even while we know the sunrise has happened before, still, the dawn's light still brings its surprises, and the new day asks and asks again, each morning, in an eternal succession to be sure, what always is its own question. But these, alas, are nearly wholly concentric with all scholars of our subject!

That is not a subtle matter. The authorship determined to

work on some tractates, not on others, first of all deciding to deal with thirty-nine tractates and to ignore twenty-three. Whether or not, as a matter of hypothesis, a system of applied reason and sustained, rigorously rational inquiry can ever coexist with an agglutinative process of sedimentary formation such as the picture of the formation of tradition evokes, is not at stake in these judgments. Whether, in theory, such a thing as pure logic deriving sustenance from not free oxygen but the accumulated nutrients of manure, in the case at hand, is not germane. But I think the issue worth pursuing on a broader front than this one. The Bavli's authorship thus solved the problem of receiving a tradition and at the same time presenting one's own, fresh answer to questions urgent in one's own time. A different mode of receiving and organizing a tradition is represented by the Bible, created by Christian intellectuals in late antiquity.

Part Three:

The Conflict of System and Tradition: The Two Resolutions of the West

CHAPTER FOURTEEN

BAVLI VS. BIBLE
SYSTEM AND IMPUTED TRADITION
VS. TRADITION AND IMPUTED SYSTEM

Through an exercise in comparison between Judaic and Christian system-building, let us now gain perspective on the Judaic problem of continuity and change in the life of intellect, yielding the solution, through the Bavli, of what I have called, with intended irony, "the *traditional* system." In the case of the mind of Judaism represented by the intellects of the Dual Torah, the system came in three parts, the Pentateuch, the Mishnah, and, in the present context, the Bavli. How to relate the three systems? It was — as we know — by forming the final statement that the Bavli's authorship wished to make into the form of a commentary on the Mishnah and on Scripture alike. The independent act of selectivity of passages requiring comment formed a principal intellectual labor of system-building. In the case of the Christian mind, where do we look for a counterpart labor of system-building through selectivity? The answer, of course, is dictated by the form of the question. We turn to the work of canonization of available writings into the Bible. There we see the counterpart, the making of choices, the setting forth of a single statement. When we compare the systemic structures represented by the Bavli and the Bible, therefore, we can appreciate how to quite distinct groups of intellectuals worked out solutions to a single problem, and did so, as a matter of fact, through pretty much the same medium, namely, the making of reasoned choices.

We shall now see that the Bavli's was not the only solution to the problem of cultural continuity within a cogent community. For imputing the standing of tradition to what was in fact an original and fresh system has an opposite. It is to gather together traditions and to impose upon them the form and structure of a system. And that is the way of holding things together in a stable composite that Christian intellectuals of the second and third centuries found in their question, out of writings deemed authoritative, of a single Christian truth, that is to say, what we should call a system. The comparison of the way of the Bavli to the manner of the Bible is apt not only because both led to a solution of a single perennial problem of on-going society facing the advent of the permanently-new. There is a second reason to undertake precisely the comparison before us.

It is the simple fact that, in the study of the formation of the intellect of Judaism within the history of Judaism, the ineluctable source of comparisons derives from Christianity, because all Judaic and Christian systems appeal to the same originating scriptures held authoritative or holy, namely, the Written Torah for the Judaism of the Dual Torah, the Old Testament for the all Orthodox and Catholic Christianity. They commonly do so, moreover, in pretty much the same way, that is to say, by quoting verses of ancient Israel's Scripture as proof-texts for their respective propositions. Implicit is the same position, that the (selected) Scripture of ancient Israel bore probative authority in disposing of claims of the faith. And that simple fact further defines the point of comparison. To specify what I deem comparable in the two traditions, I point to the simple fact that each defines its authority by appeal to revelation, and both religious traditions know precisely the locus of revelation.

The comparison at hand may be simply stated. The Bible, for Christianity, and the Bavli, for Judaism, have not only formed the court of final appeal in issues of doctrine and (for Judaism) normative instruction on correct deed as well. Each writing in its way has solved for its family of religious systems a fundamental dilemma of intellect and culture facing both sets of systems. But, while the comparison is not only justified but demanded, still, the Bavli and the Bible present us with quite different kinds of documents. And in the differences we see the choices people made when confronting pretty much the same problem. For, in late antiquity, from the second through the fourth centuries for Orthodox, Catholic Christianity, and from the second through the seventh centuries for the Judaism of the Dual Torah, the Judaic and Christian intellectuals sorted out the complex problem of relating the worlds of the then-moderns to the words of the ancients. Both groups of intellectuals then claimed to present enduring traditions, a fundament of truth revealed of old. But both sets of thinkers also brought to realization systematic and philosophical statements, which begin in first principles and rise in steady and inexorable logic to final conclusions: compositions of proportion, balance, cogency, and order.

Christianity finds in the Bible, meaning the Old Testament and the New Testament, the statement of the faith by the authority of God. And however diverse the readings of the Bible, Christian theologians, Catholic (Roman or Greek or Armenian or Russian in language) and Protestant alike define the foundations of all divine knowledge as the simple fact that there is a pattern of Christian truth, awaiting discovery and demonstration. So all Christianities appeal not to diverse traditions, insusceptible of harmonization, but to a Christian truth, the idea of orthodoxy, if not to the same Orthodoxy. Accordingly, as we shall see, Christianities – Christian systems in the language of this book — concur that there is more than tradition, there is also what we should call system, one Christian system, whatever it may be. And the Bible forms the statement of that system, however we choose to read it. Accordingly, the Bible for all Christianities forms traditions into a single system.

For its part, the regnant Judaism from antiquity to our own day, the Judaism of the Dual Torah, presents itself not as an invented system of the sixth century, elaborated, adapted, expanded, revised from then to now, but as tradition, specifically, the increment of truth revealed by God to Moses and handed on, generation by generation, with each generation contributing to the sedimentary legacy of Sinai. And that Judaism has identified in the Bavli, the Talmud of Babylonia, the summa of the Torah of Sinai, joining as it does the Written Torah, encompassing what Christianity knows as the Old Testament, and the Oral Torah, commencing with the Mishnah. The systematic character of the statement of the Bavli, the cogency of its logic and its systemic statement, the paramount and blatant character of its self-evidently valid answer to its sustaining and critical question — these facts require no elaboration at the present point in the unfolding argument of this book. It suffices only to repeat that the Bavli represents system as tradition. Comparison requires also observing contrasts, and, as a matter of fact, the points of difference are determined by the shared morphology: the Bible and the Bavli are very different ways of setting forth a system. Each represents its components in a distinctive manner, the one by preserving their autonomy and calling the whole a system, the other by obscuring their originally autonomous and independent character and imparting to the whole the form of tradition. The upshot may be simple stated. The Bavli presents a system and to it through the operative logics imputes the standing of tradition . The Bible sets forth diverse and unsystematic traditions, received writings from we know not where, and to those traditions, through the act of canonization, imputes the character and structure of (a) system.

To unpack these generalizations, let us turn back to the literary media in which the intellects of the two communities of intellectuals set forth their system as traditions or their traditions as system: the Bavli and the Bible, respectively. We wish specifically to see how each of these monuments of mind works out its own system and, consequently, also, accomplishes the consequent tasks at hand, first, the sorting out the issue of choosing a logic of cogent discourse to serve

the interests of the system, second, the situating of the system in relationship to received and authoritative, prior systemic statements. In the case of the Bavli, our point of entry was the identification of the odd mixture of logics utilized by the framers of the system as a whole. Why did they find it necessary to resort to that mixture? It was dictated by the character of the Mishnah. Not only so, but the logics used for cogent discourse themselves conveyed the systemic message, once again, dictated by the intent of the system-builders. We now realize that the Bavli's framers wished to present a system in the disguise of a tradition, and hence set a high priority upon relating their ideas to received writings. But when they read the Mishnah, they found a writing with a quite opposite intent, which was, as we remember, to appeal for power of persuasion not to (mere) authority but to the compelling force of logic, structure, order. When we understand the character of the Mishnah and its relationship to the immediately-prior system its authorship recognized, which was the Pentateuch (and Scripture as a whole), we shall grasp the choices confronting the Bavli's
framers. The issue then was authority, and the position of the authorship of one system simply contradict the datum of the authorship of the successor-system. What the Bavli's framers did, then, was to subvert the received system by imposing upon it precisely the character the Mishnah's authorship had rejected, namely, that of a commentary to Scripture, a secondary expansion of Scripture. And — it would inexorably follow — quite by the way, the Bavli's framers then adopted for their own system that same form that they again and again imposed upon the Mishnah's system.

    And that brings us directly to the problem of authority in the Mishnah. The issue presented by the Mishnah, which the Bavli in its form is arranged to serve as a vast exegesis, derives from the form and character of the Mishnah itself. For the Mishnah, as we saw, utilized a single logic to set forth a system that, in form as in inner structure, stood wholly autonomous and independent, a statement unto itself, with scarcely a ritual obeisance to any prior system. As soon as the Mishnah made its appearance, therefore, the vast labor of not only explaining its meaning but especially justifying its authority was sure to get under way. For the Mishnah presented one striking problem in particular. It rarely cited scriptural authority for its rules. Instead, it followed the inexorable authority of logic, specifically, the inner logic of a topic, which dictated the order of thought and defined the generative problematic that instructed its authors on what they wanted to know about a particular topic. These intellectual modalities in their nature lay claim to an independence of mind, even when, in point of fact, the result of thought is a repetition of what Scripture itself says. Omitting scriptural proof texts therefore represents both silence and signals its statement. For that act of omission bore the implicit claim to an authority independent of Scripture, an authority deriving from logic working within its own inner tensions and appealing to tests of reason and sound argument. In that striking fact the document set a new course for itself. But its authorship raised problems for those who would apply its law to Israel's life.

What choices lay before the intellect of Judaism as it came to realization among system-builders? From the formation of ancient Israelite Scripture into a holy book in Judaism, in the aftermath of the return to Zion and the creation of the Torah-book in Ezra's time (ca. 450 B.C.) the established canon of revelation (whatever its contents) coming generations routinely set their ideas into relationship with Scripture. This they did by citing proof-texts alongside their own rules. Otherwise, in the setting of Israelite culture, the new writings could find no ready hearing. Over the six hundred years from the formation of the Torah of "Moses" in the time of Ezra, from ca. 450 B.C. to ca. A.D. 200, four conventional ways to accommodate new writings — new "tradition" — to the established canon of received Scripture had come to the fore.

First and simplest, a writer would sign a famous name to his book, attributing his ideas to Enoch, Adam, Jacob's sons, Jeremiah, Baruch, and any number of others, down to Ezra. But the Mishnah bore no such attribution, e.g., to Moses. Implicitly, to be sure, the statement of M. Avot 1:1, "Moses received Torah from Sinai" carried the further notion that sayings of people on the list of authorities from Moses to nearly their own day derived from God's revelation at Sinai.

But no one made that premise explicit before the time of the Bavli of the Land of Israel.

Second, an authorship might also imitate the style of biblical Hebrew and so try to creep into the canon by adopting the cloak of Scripture. But the Mishnah's authorship ignores biblical syntax and style.

Third, an author would surely claim his work was inspired by God, a new revelation for an open canon. But, as we realize, that claim makes no explicit impact on the Mishnah.

Fourth, at the very least, someone would link his opinions to biblical verses through the exegesis of the latter in line with the former so Scripture would validate his views. The authorship of the Mishnah did so only occasionally, but far more commonly stated on its own authority whatever rules it proposed to lay down.

The Hebrew of the Mishnah complicated the problem, because it is totally different from the Hebrew of the Hebrew Scriptures. Its verb, for instance, makes provision for more than completed or continuing action, for which the biblical Hebrew verb allows, but also for past and future times, subjunctive and indicative voices, and much else. The syntax is Indo-European, in that we can translate the word order of the Mishnah into any Indo-European language and come up with perfect sense. None of that crabbed imitation of biblical Hebrew, that makes the Dead Sea scrolls an embarrassment to read, characterizes the Hebrew of the Mishnah. Mishnaic style is elegant, subtle, exquisite in its sensitivity to word-order and repetition, balance, pattern.

The solution to the problem of the authority of the Mishnah, that is to say, its relationship to Scripture, was worked out in the period after the closure of the Mishnah. Since no one now could credibly claim to sign the name of Ezra or Adam to a book of this kind, and since biblical Hebrew had provided no apologetic aesthetics whatever, the only options lay elsewhere. The two were, first, to provide a myth of the origin of the contents of the Mishnah, and, second, to link each allegation of the Mishnah, through processes of biblical (not Mishnaic) exegesis, to verses of the Scriptures. These two procedures, together, would establish for the Mishnah that standing that the uses to which the document was to be put demanded for it: a place in the canon of Israel, a legitimate relationship to the Torah of Moses. There were several ways in which the work went forward. These are represented by diverse documents that succeeded and dealt with the Mishnah. Let me now state the three principal possibilities. (1) The Mishnah required no systematic support through exegesis of Scripture in light of Mishnaic laws. (2) The Mishnah by itself provided no reliable information and all of its propositions demanded linkage to Scripture, to which the Mishnah must be shown to be subordinate and secondary. (3) The Mishnah is an autonomous document, but closely correlated with Scripture.

The first extreme is represented by the Abot, ca. 250 A.D., which represents the authority of the sages cited in Abot as autonomous of Scripture. Those authorities in Abot do not cite verses of Scripture but what they say does constitute a statement of the Torah. There can be no clearer way of saying that what these authorities present in and of itself falls into the classification of the Torah. The authorship of the Tosefta, ca. 400 A.D., takes the middle position. It very commonly cites a passage of the Mishnah and then adds to that passage an appropriate proof-text. That is a quite common mode of supplementing the Mishnah. The mediating view is further taken by the Yerushalmi and the Bavli, ca. 400-600. In line with the view of the Yerushalmi's authorship, that of the Bavli developed a well-crafted theory of the Mishnah and its relationship to Scripture. Each rule of the Mishnah is commonly introduced, in the exegesis supplied by the two Talmuds, with the question, "What is the source of this statement?" And the answer invariably is, "As it is said," or "...written," with a verse of Scripture, that is, the Written Torah, then cited. The upshot is that the source of the rules of the Mishnah (and other writings) is Scripture, not free-standing logic. The far extreme — everything in the Mishnah makes sense only as a (re)statement of Scripture or upon Scripture's authority — is taken by the Sifra, a post-Mishnaic compilation of exegeses on Leviticus, redacted at an indeterminate point, perhaps about 300 A.D. The Sifra systematically challenges reason (=the Mishnah), unaided by revelation (that is, exegesis of Scripture), to sustain positions taken by the Mishnah, which is cited verbatim, and everywhere proves that it cannot be done.

The final and normative solution to the problem of the authority of the Mishnah worked out in the third and fourth centuries produced the myth of the Dual Torah, oral and written, which formed the indicative and definitive trait of the Judaism that emerged from late antiquity. Tracing the unfolding of that myth leads us deep into the processes by which that Judaism took shape. The Bavli knows the theory that there is a tradition separate from, and in addition to, the Written Torah. This tradition it knows as "the teachings of scribes." The Mishnah is identified as the collection of those teachings only by implication in the Bavli. I cannot point to a single passage in which explicit judgment upon the character and status of the Mishnah as a complete document is laid down. Nor is the Mishnah treated as a symbol or called "the Oral Torah." But there is ample evidence, once again implicit in what happens to the Mishnah in the Bavli, to allow a reliable description of how the Bavli's founders viewed the Mishnah. That view may be stated very simply. The Mishnah rarely cites verses of Scripture in support of its propositions. The Bavli routinely adduces Scriptural bases for the Mishnah's laws. The Mishnah seldom undertakes the exegesis of verses of Scripture for any purpose. The Bavli consistently investigates the meaning of verses of Scripture, and does so for a variety of purposes. Accordingly, the Bavli, subordinate as it is to the Mishnah, regards the Mishnah as subordinate to, and contingent upon, Scripture. That is why, in the Bavli's view, the Mishnah requires the support of proof-texts of Scripture. By itself, the Mishnah exercises no autonomous authority and enjoys no independent standing or norm-setting status.

And this brings us back, by a circuitous and somewhat long, even tedious, route, to the Bavli's authorship's explanation of its own position in relationship to the received "tradition," which is to say, to prior systemic statements, the Pentateuch's and the Mishnah's in particular. Their solution to the problem of the standing and authority of the Mishnah dictated their answer to the question of the representation, within a received tradition, of their own system as well. It was through pretending to speak only by a phrase by phrase commentary that the Bavli's authorship justified the Mishnah as tradition and represented it as a secondary elaboration of Scripture or as invariably resting on the authority of Scripture. And that same form, in the nature of things, bore the burden of their systemic statement as well.

That form, as we realize, does what can be done to represent sentences of the Mishnah as related to sentences of Scripture. That mode of writing, moreover, accomplished what we may call the dismantling or deconstruction of the system of the Mishnah and the reconstruction of its bits and pieces into the system of the Bavli. For, as even the little sample in the preceding chapter has shown us, the Bavli's authorship never represented the Mishnah's system whole and complete, and rarely acknowledged that the Mishnah consisted of more than discrete statements, to be related to some larger cogent law that transcended the Mishnah. Having represented the Mishnah as it did, therefore, the Bavli's authorship quite naturally chose to represent its own system in the same way, that is to say, as a mere elaboration of a received tradition, a stage in the sedimentary and incremental process by which the Torah continued to come down from Sinai. And for that purpose, I hardly need to add, the mixed logics embodied in the joining of philosophical and propositional statements on the principle of fixed association to a prior text served exceedingly well. That explains how, in the Bavli, we have, in the (deceptive) form of a tradition, what is in fact an autonomous system, connected with prior systems but not continuous with them.

The authorship represented their own statement of an ethos, ethics, and defined social entity, precisely as they did the received ones, the whole forming a single, seamless Torah revealed by God to Moses at Sinai. So much for a system to which the standing of tradition is imputed through formal means. And that decision concerning the literary presentation of a system would dictate the shape of the intellect of Judaism, therefore the morphology and structure of the culture of Judaism, from then to nearly the present. That culture would prize tradition, deny innovation, insist upon the authority of the Torah, even as each generation, in its turn, did pretty much whatever it chose to do. The form of tradition would mask the advent of sequential and mutually incompatible systems and join them into a secure structure, resting squarely on Sinai.

When we come to the counterpart religious world, we confront Christian intellectuals, dealing also with the inheritance of ancient Israel's scriptures facing the same problem, as I said at the outset. The parallel is exact in yet another aspect. Just as the authorship of the Bavli received not only what they came to call the Written Torah, but also the Mishnah and other writings that had attained acceptance, hence authority, from the closure of the Mishnah to their own day, so too did the Christian intellectuals inherit more than the Old Testament. They too had in hand a variety of authoritative documents, to which the inspiration of the Holy Spirit was imputed. So they confronted the same problem as faced the authorship of the Bavli, and it was in pretty much the same terms: namely, how to sort out received documents, each of which making its own statement take up a different problem and follow a different solution to that problem. The issue of the authority of contradictory traditions defined the task at hand.

What the Christian intellectuals, working over several centuries from ca. 100 through ca. 400, did was to join together the received writings as autonomous books but to impute to the whole the standing of a cogent statement, a single and harmonious Christian truth. This they did in the work of making the biblical canon. Joining diverse traditions into one, single, uniform, and, therefore, (putatively) harmonious Bible: God's word. And, once more, that explains my view that the Christian solution to the problem of making a statement but also situating that system in relationship to received tradition is to be characterized as imputing system to discrete traditions through a declared canon. Thus, as in the title of this chapter, the comparison of the solutions that would prevail, respectively, in Judaism's Bavli and Christianity's Bible, are characterized as a system to which the standing of tradition is imputed, as against traditions, to which the form of a single system is, through the canonization of scriptures as The Bible, imputed. The legitimacy of my comparing the two intellects through their ultimate statements, the Bavli and the Bible, seems to me sustained by the simple theological judgment of Turner:

> The mind of the Church [in making the canon] was guided by criteria rationally devised and flexibly applied. There is no dead hand in the production of the Canon; there is rather the living action of the Holy Spirit using as He is wont the full range of the continuing life of the Church to achieve His purposes in due season.[3]

I can find no better language to state, in a way interior to a system, the claim that a writing or a set of writings constitutes a system: a way of life, a world-view, an address to a particular social entity. This too is made explicit by Turner, who I take to be a thoroughly reliable representative of Christian theology on the subject:

> There can be no doubt that the Bible is fundamentally an orthodox book, sufficient if its teaching is studied as a whole to lead to orthodox conclusions...The Biblical data insist upon arranging themselves in certain theological patterns and cannot be forced into other moulds without violent distortion. That is the point of a famous simile of St. Irenaeus. The teaching of Scripture can be compared to a mosaic of the head of a king, but the heretics break up the pattern and reassemble it in the form of a dog or a fox...

A master of the Bavli could not have said it better in claiming both the systemic character, and the traditional standing, of his statement.[4]

---

[3] H. E. W. Turner, *The Pattern of Christian Truth. A Study of the Relations between Orthodoxy and Heresy in the Early Church. Bampton Lectures, 1954* (London, 1954: A. R. Mowbray & Co., Ltd.). I do claim that my representation of matters accords with Turner's chapter, "Orthodoxy and the Bible," pp. 241ff.

[4] In laying matters out, I avoid entering the issues debated by Walter Bauer, *Orthodoxy and Heresy in Earliest Christianity* (Philadelphia, 1971: Fortress), translation of *Rechtgläubigkeit und Ketzerei im ältesten Christentum* (1934, supplemented by Georg Strecker, 1964), edited by Robert A. Kraft and Gerhard Krodel, and H. E. W. Turner,

Let me hasten to qualify the comparison at hand. In claiming that a single problem, one of relating a system to tradition, for Judaism, or traditions into a system, for Christianity, found two solutions in the Bavli and the Bible, respectively, I do not for one minute suggest that the two groups of intellectuals were thinking along the same lines at all. Quite to the contrary, the comparison derives from a different standpoint altogether. For, if we ask, when the Christian theologians worked out the idea of "the Bible," consisting of "the Old Testament and the New Testament," and when the Judaic theologians worked out the idea of "the Dual Torah," consisting of "the Written Torah and the Oral Torah," did each group propose to answer a question confronting the other group as well? we answer negative. For, as a matter of fact, each party pursued a problem particular to the internal logic and life of its own group. They were different people talking about the same thing to different people. True, as a matter of necessity, each party had to designate within the larger corpus of scriptures deriving from ancient Israel those writings that it regarded as authoritative, therefore divinely revealed. But did the one side do so for the same reasons, and within the same sort of theological logic, that they other did? Each party had further to explain to itself the end-result, that is, the revealed words as a whole? What are they all together, all at once? The one party characterized the whole as a single Bible, book, piece of writing, and the other party characterized the whole as a single Torah, revelation, in two media, the one, writing, the other, memory. But these characterizations of the result of revelation, that is, of the canon, hardly constitute intersecting statements. The reason that, for Christianity, traditions became a system, as Turner testifies was the intent and the outcome, derives from the life of the Church, not from the issues of culture in its relationship to change, system in its realization in the logic of cogent discourse, such

---

The Pattern of Christian Truth. A Study of the Relations between Orthodoxy and Heresy in the Early Church. Bampton Lectures, 1954 (London, 1954: A. R. Mowbray & Co., Ltd.). I do claim that my representation of matters accords with Turner's chapter, "Orthodoxy and the Bible," pp. 241ff.

as I have framed here.

That is indeed what makes the matter so intensely interesting even now, namely, the capacity of rigorously disciplined theologians to state in terms of their language and the compelling logic particular to their intellects what we for our part perceive as not logical at all, but as (merely) adventitious perplexities of the ongoing social world of culture. That is to say, in simple language, things happen. People write books. Other people believe in those books. There need not be a logic to form of those diverse writings a single harmonious statement, a system, a stunning answer to an ineluctable question. But the Christian theologians took a sizable corpus of unrelated documents and turned them into the Bible, and they furthermore imputed to that Bible the character of a system and even claimed to uncover, within the Bible, structure, order, proportion, harmony, and, by the way, doctrine, hence: Christian truth. And the Judaic sages did no less, but they did it with different kinds of writings, for different reasons, and in a different way. The issue framed as discovering the pattern of Christian truth addressed the authority of received writings and their harmony, and that issue, I maintain, faced the Judaic sages in their encounter with the system of the Mishnah. But for both Christian and Judaic intellectuals, the issues at hand derived from the very nature of the social world: its continuing to evolve in patterns not imposed by the logic of an inherited system, but determined only by the inexorable but immediate confrontation of the latest generation with the questions imposed upon it by the advent of a fresh tomorrow.

Let us briefly review the formation of the Bible, that is to say, in literary terms the reorganization of received, that is, traditional writings into a system, that is, as Turner says, a canon, a pattern of Christian truth. That canonical process in small dimension stood for a broader cultural process of the formation of the Christian civilization of the West, based as it was on the Bible and on the processes of cultural elaboration and adaptation that commenced in the creation of the Bible. Seeing the canonical process as a microcosm of the formation of the Christian civilization, we can grasp in perspective also what is at stake in the counterpart process of the making of a traditional system as the foundation of the Judaic civilization in the same time and place.

In the centuries after the Gospels were written, the Church had to come to a decision on whether, in addition to the Scriptures of ancient Israel, there would be a further corpus of authoritative writing. The Church affirmed that there would be, and the New Testament as counterpart to the Old Testament evolved into the canon. When we speak of canon, we refer, in Childs' words, to "the process of theological interpretation by a faith community [that] left its mark on a literary text which did not continue to evolve and which became the normative interpretation of the events to which it bore witness for those identifying with that religious community."[5]

Christians from the very beginning revered the Hebrew Scriptures as "the Old Testament," regarding it as their sacred book. They denied the Jews any claim to the book, accusing them of misinterpreting it. The Old Testament served, in Harnack's words, to prove "that the appearance and the entire history of Jesus had been predicted hundreds and even thousands of years ago; and further, that the founding of the New People which was to be fashioned out of all the nations upon earth had from the very beginning been prophesied and prepared for."[6] The text of the Hebrew Scriptures supplied proofs for various propositions of theology, law, and liturgy. It served as a source of precedents: "if God had praised or punished this or that in the past, how much more...are we to look for similar treatment from him, we who are now living in the last days and who have received 'the calling of promise.'" Even after the rise of the New Testament, much of the Old Testament held its own. And, Harnack concludes, "The New testament as a whole did not generally play the same role as the Old Testament in the mission and practice of the church."

In the beginning the Church did not expect the canon — now meaning only the Hebrew Scripture — to grow through Christian additions. But then, in those same formative centuries, the Church

---

[5] Childs: Brevard S. Childs, *The New Testament as Canon*, p. 26
[6] ; Harnack: Adolf Harnack, *Mission and Expansion of Christianity*, pp. 283-4.

also did not anticipate that it would bear responsibility for the definition of the state and the organization of civilization. It bore no world-historical and social vision, and its perspective was that of a small group within society, not the governing and nurturing agency of society that it would become after Constantine and until 1787 (for the United States of America) and 1789 (For Europe). For, as Cross says, "In the new covenant the sole complement to the Word in the Torah was the Word made flesh in Christ." So it would be some time before a Christian canon encompassing not only the received writings but the writings of the new age would come into being. For, until the time at hand, the Bible of the Church consisted of the Hebrew Scriptures, "the Old Testament." Before Marcion the Bible of the Church was the Hebrew Scriptures, pure and simple. While Filson assigns to the years between 160 and 175 the crystallization of the concept of the canon, the process came to the end by the end of the fourth century. Filson states, "There was no longer any wide dispute over the right of any of our twenty-seven books to a place in the New Testament canon." What was not a settled question for Eusebius, in 330, had been worked out in the next span of time. So, in general, when we take up the issue of the canon of Christianity, we find ourselves in the third and fourth centuries.

The bulk of the work was complete by 200, with details under debate for another two hundred years. The orthodoxy in which "the canon of an Old and a New Testament was firmly laid down," did not come into being overnight. From the time of Irenaeus the church affirmed the bipartite Christian Bible, containing the Old, and, parallel with this and controlling it, the New Testament. But what was to be in the New Testament, and when were the limits of the canon decided? Von Campenhausen concludes the description for us:

> [The Muratorian fragment] "displays for the first time the concept of a collection of New Testament scriptures, which has deliberately been closed, and the individual books of which are regarded as 'accepted' and ecclesiastically 'sanctified,' that is to say....they have been 'incorporated' into the valid corpus. We have thus arrived at the end of the long journey which leads

to a New Testament thought of as 'canonical' in the strict sense. Only one thing is still lacking: the precise name for this collection, which will make it possible to refer to the new Scripture as a unity and thus at one and the same time both to distinguish it from the old Scriptures and combine it with them in a new totality...This is the last feature still wanting to the accomplishment of the bipartite Christian Bible.

When does the Old Testament join the New as the Bible? Von Campenhausen makes a striking point. There was no need to look for a single name for the entire document. There was no such thing as an Old Testament or a New Testament as a single physical entity. To the eye the whole canon was still fragmented into a series of separate rolls or volumes." Von Campenhausen makes a still more relevant point:

> There was no reason why in themselves the two parts of the Bible should not have different names. In the early period one possibility suggested itself almost automatically: if one had the New and the Old Testament in mind, one could speak of the 'Gospel' and the 'Law.'

The use of "Old" and "New" Testament represents a particular theology. It was from the beginning of the third century that Scripture for orthodox Christianity consisted of an Old and a New Testament. So, we conclude, "Both the Old and the New Testaments had in essence already reached their final form and significance around the year 200." The authority of the Bible, for Christianity, rested on the reliability of the biblical record of ,the predictions of Christ in the prophets and the testimony to Christ of the apostles.

The biblical component of the "canon of truth" proved contingent, not absolute and dominant. So much for the Christian canon: traditions made into a system, writings into the Bible.

We began with a labor of comparison. We do well to remind ourselves that we compare things that are really not like one another. For we now realize that the issues important to the Judaism of the sages were in no way consubstantial with the issues at hand. None of the cited theological precipitants for the canonical process in a Judaic formulation played any role I can discern in the theory of the Torah in two media. The myth of the Dual Torah, which functioned as a canonical process, validating as it did the writings of sages as part of Torah from Sinai, derives from neither the analogy to the Old Testament process nor — to begin with — from the narrow issue of finding a place for the specific writings of rabbis within the larger Torah, and, it follows, we cannot refer to "the Bible" when we speak of Judaism.

When scholars of the formation of the canon of Christianity use the word canon, they mean, first, the recognition of sacred Scripture, over and beyond the (received) Hebrew Scriptures, second, the identification of writings revered within the Church as canonical, hence authoritative, third, the recognition that these accepted writings formed a Scripture, which, fourth, served as the counterpart to the Hebrew Scriptures, hence, fifth, the formation of the Bible as the Old and New Testaments. Now, as a matter of fact, none of these categories, stage by stage, corresponds in any way to the processes in the unfolding of the holy books of the sages, which I shall now describe in terms of Torah. But the word "Torah" in the context of the writings of the sages at hand in no way forms that counterpart to the word "canon" as used (quite correctly) by Childs, von Campenhausen, and others, and, moreover the word "Bible" and the word "Torah" in no way speak of the same thing, I mean, they do not refer to the same category or classification.

But the difference is the very point of the comparison, for, after all, the generative problematic was the same: holding together received conceptions in a contemporary statement, answering new questions out of inherited truths, setting forth a system in such a way as to affirm its traditional authority (Judaism), setting forth tradition in such a way as to claim its systemic harmony (Christianity). So the differences require underlining. And this requires a set of banal observations. First, the statement of the Bavli is not a canonical system at all. For in the mode of presentation of the Bavli's system, as a matter of fact, revelation does not close or reach conclusion. God speaks all the time, through the sages. Representing the whole as "Torah" means that the Bavli speaks a tradition formed in God's revelation of God's will to Moses, our rabbi. Ancient Israel's scriptures fall into the category of Torah, but they do not fill that category up. Other writings fall into that same category. By contrast canon refers to particular books that enjoy a distinctive standing, Torah refers to various things that fall into a particular classification. There is a second, still more fundamental difference between Bible and Bavli. The Christian canon reached closure with the Bible: Old and New Testaments. The Judaic Torah never closed: revelation of Torah continued. The Torah is not the Bible, and the Bible is not the Torah. The difference in process leading to Bible and Bavli, respectively, has been spelled out in my brief summaries of two distinct histories. The Bible emerges from the larger process of establishing Church order and doctrine. The Torah ("Oral and Written") for its part derives from the larger process of working out in relationship to the Pentateuchal system the authority and standing of two successive and connected systems that had followed, the Mishnah, then the Bavli. But the problem solved for Christianity by the Bible and for Judaism by the Bavli is one and the same problem. And that is one not of literature, let alone mere logic of cogent discourse. It is the problem of relating on-going history to a well-composed culture, change to continuity, the newest generation to the enduring social world, and, in the deep reality of the heart and soul, daughters to mothers and sons to fathers.

    Let me therefore conclude at the point at which I commenced, with the observation that thought proceeds always in a context, whether one of logic and process or proposition and proportion and composition. And context always is social. A long-standing problem faced all system-builders in the tradition that commenced with the Pentateuch. From that original system onward, system-builders, both in Judaism and, as we now realize, in Christianity, would have to represent their system not as an original statement on its own, but as part of a tradition of revealed truth. Not only so, but in the passage of time and in the accumulation of writing, intellectuals, both Christian and Judaic, would have to work out logics that would permit cogent discourse within the inherited traditions and with them. In the Christian case, the solution to the problem lay in accepting as canonical a variety of documents, each with its own logic. We note, for instance, that extraordinarily cogent communication could be accomplished, in some Christian writings, through symbol and not through proposition at all. Christian writings exhibit each its own coherent logical principles of cogency, with the making of connections and the drawing of conclusions fully consistent throughout.

The final solution of the canon sidestepped the problem of bringing these logics together within a single statement. If diverse logics work, each for its own authoritative writing, then I really do not have to effect coherence among diverse logics at all, and the canon, the conception of The Bible, would impose from without a cogency of discourse difficult to discern in the interior of the canonical writings. That decision would then dictate the future of the Christian intellectual enterprise: to explore the underbrush of the received writing and to straighten out the tangled roots. No wonder, then, that, in philosophy, culminating in the return to Athens, the Christian mind would recover that glory of logical and systematic order denied it in the dictated canon, the Bible. But the canon did solve the problem that faced the heirs to a rather odd corpus of writing. Ignoring logic as of no account, accepting considerable diversity in modes of making connections and drawing conclusions, the traditional solution represented a better answer than the librarians of the Essenes at Qumran had found, which was to set forth (so far as matters now seem at any rate) neither a system nor a canon.

The Bavli's authorship was the first in the history of Judaism, encompassing Christianity in its earliest phases, to take up, in behalf of its distinct and distinctive system, a position of relationship with the received heritage of tradition, with a corpus of truth assigned to God's revelation to Moses at Sinai. The framers of the Pentateuch did not do so; rather they said what they wrote was the work of God, dictating to Moses at Sinai. The Essene librarians at Qumran did not do so. They collected this and that, never even pretending that everything fit together in some one way, not as commentary to Scripture (though some wrote commentaries), not as systemic statements (though the

Rabbinic Judaism's Generative Logic: Volume Two   143

library included such statements, as we noticed), and not as a canon (unless everything we find in the detritus forms a canon by definition). The authorship of the Mishnah did not do so. Quite to the contrary, it undertook the pretense that, even when Scripture supplied facts and even dictated the order of the facts, their writing was new and fresh and their own.

No wonder that the Mishnah's authorship resorted to its own logic to make its own statement in its own language and for its own purposes. No wonder, too, that the hubris of the Mishnah's authorship provoked the systematic demonstration of the dependence of the Mishnah on Scripture — but also the allegation that the Mishnah stood as an autonomous statement, another Torah, the oral one, co-equal with the Written Torah. The hubris of the great intellects of Judaic and Christian antiquity, the daring authorships of the Pentateuch and the Mishnah, the great ecclesiastical minds behind the Bible, reached its boldest realization in the Bavli. This authorship accomplished, as we have seen, through its ingenious joining of two distinct and contradictory logics of cogent discourse the statement of the Torah in its own rhetoric, following its own logic, and in accord with its own designated topical program. But hubris is not the sole trait that characterizes the mind of Judaism, encompassing its Christian successors, in classical times.

There is a second trait common to them all. It is that in all systemic constructions and statements the issues of logic responded to the systemic imperative and in no way dictated the shape and structure of that imperative. The system invariably proves to be prior, recapitulating itself, also, in its logic. And however diverse the issues addressed by various systems made up by the mind of Judaism in classical times, all had to address a single question natural to the religious ecology in which Judaic systems flourished. That question, in the aftermath of the Pentateuchal system, concerned how people could put together in a fresh construction and a composition of distinctive proportions a statement that purported to speak truth to a social entity that, in the nature of things, already had truth. This framing of the issue of how system contradicts tradition, how the logic that tells me to make a connection of this to that, but not to the other thing, and to draw from that connection one conclusion, rather than some other — that framing of the issue places intellect, the formation of mind and modes of thought squarely into the on-going processes dictated by the givens of society.

Why then characterize the Bavli's system-builders as the climax of the hubris of the intellect of Judaism? Because the Bavli's authorship was the first in the history of Judaism, encompassing Christianity in its earliest phases, to take up, in behalf of its distinct and distinctive system, a considered position of relationship with the received heritage of tradition, with a corpus of truth assigned to God's revelation to Moses at Sinai. Four centuries after the Mishnah, in their mind eighteen centuries after God revealed the Torah to Moses at Mount Sinai, the Bavli's authorship remade the two received systems, the Pentateuchal and the Mishnaic. In its own rhetoric, in accord with its own topical program, appealing to a logic unique to itself among all the minds of Judaisms in ancient times, that authorship presented the Torah of Sinai precisely as it wished to represent it. And it did so defiantly, not discretely and by indirection. Not merely alleging that Moses had written it all down, like the Pentateuchal compilers, nor modestly identifying with the direction of the Holy Spirit the choices that it made, like the Christians responsible for making the Bible, nor even, as with the framers of the Mishnah, sedulously sidestepping, in laconic and disingenuous innocence, the issue of authority and tradition entirely. Quite the opposite, the Bavli's intellectuals took over the entire tradition, scriptural and Mishnaic alike, chose what they wanted, tacked on to the selected passages their own words in their own way, and then put it all out as a single statement of their own.

True, they claimed for their system the standing of a mere amplification of that tradition,. But, as a matter of fact, they did say it all in their own words and they did set forth the whole of their statement in their own way, and — as above all — without recapitulating the received choices of ignoring or merely absorbing the received revelation, they represented as the one whole Torah revealed by God to Moses, our rabbi, at Sinai what they themselves had made up, and they made it stick. And that, I think, is the supreme hubris of the mind of Judaism from the beginnings, in the Pentateuch, to the conclusion and climax in the Bavli. I like to think that that hubris of theirs at least for the beauty of it explains the success of what they made up, on the simple principle, the more daring, the more plausible. For theirs was the final realization and statement in the formation of the intellect of Judaism. Their mode of making connections and drawing conclusions defined, from then to now, the systems and the traditions of Judaisms.

WITHDRAWN